Practice Guideline

for the

Treatment of Patients With Eating Disorders

Second Edition

American Psychiatric Association

American Psychiatric Association
1400 K Street, N.W., Washington, DC 20005
www.psych.org

ISSN 1067-8743
ISBN 0-89042-314-8

TABLE OF CONTENTS

STATEMENT OF INTENT

This guideline is not intended to be construed or to serve as a standard of medical care. Standards of medical care are determined on the basis of all clinical data available for an individual case and are subject to change as scientific knowledge and technology advance and patterns evolve. These parameters of practice should be considered guidelines only. Adherence to them will not ensure a successful outcome in every case, nor should they be construed as including all proper methods of care aimed at the same results. The ultimate judgment regarding a particular clinical procedure or treatment plan must be made by the psychiatrist in light of the clinical data presented by the patient and the diagnostic and treatment options available.

This practice guideline has been developed by psychiatrists who are in active clinical practice. In addition, some contributors are primarily involved in research or other academic endeavors. It is possible that through such activities some contributors have received income related to treatments discussed in this guideline. A number of mechanisms are in place to minimize the potential for producing biased recommendations due to conflicts of interest. The guideline has been extensively reviewed by members of APA as well as by representatives from related fields. Contributors and reviewers have all been asked to base their recommendations on an objective evaluation of the available evidence. Any contributor or reviewer who has a potential conflict of interest that may bias (or appear to bias) his or her work has been asked to notify the APA Office of Quality Improvement and Psychiatric Services. This potential bias is then discussed with the work group chair and the chair of the Steering Committee on Practice Guidelines. Further action depends on the assessment of the potential bias.

This practice guideline was approved in July 1999 and was published in January 2000.

I. EXECUTIVE SUMMARY

▶ A. CODING SYSTEM

Each recommendation is identified as falling into one of three categories of endorsement, indicated by a bracketed Roman numeral following the statement. The three categories represent varying levels of clinical confidence regarding the recommendations:

[I] recommended with substantial clinical confidence.
[II] recommended with moderate clinical confidence.
[III] may be recommended on the basis of individual circumstances.

▶ B. GENERAL CONSIDERATIONS

Patients with eating disorders display a broad range of symptoms that frequently occur along a continuum between those of anorexia nervosa and bulimia nervosa. The care of patients with eating disorders involves a comprehensive array of approaches. These guidelines contain the clinical factors that need to be considered when treating a patient with anorexia nervosa or bulimia nervosa.

1. Choosing a site of treatment

Evaluation of the patient with an eating disorder prior to initiating treatment is essential for determining the appropriate setting of treatment. The most important physical parameters that affect this decision are weight and cardiac and metabolic status [I]. Patients should be psychiatrically hospitalized before they become medically unstable (i.e., display abnormal vital signs) [I]. The decision to hospitalize should be based on psychiatric, behavioral, and general medical factors [I]. These include rapid or persistent decline in oral intake and decline in weight despite outpatient or partial hospitalization interventions, the presence of additional stressors that interfere with the patient's ability to eat (e.g., intercurrent viral illnesses), prior knowledge of weight at which instability is likely to occur, or comorbid psychiatric problems that merit hospitalization.

Most patients with uncomplicated bulimia nervosa do not require hospitalization. However, the indications for hospitalization for these patients can include severe disabling symptoms that have not responded to outpatient treatment, serious concurrent general medical problems (e.g., metabolic abnormalities, hematemesis, vital sign changes, and the appearance of uncontrolled vomiting), suicidality, psychiatric disturbances that warrant hospitalization independent of the eating disorders diagnosis, or severe concurrent alcohol or drug abuse.

Factors influencing the decision to hospitalize on a psychiatric versus a general medical or adolescent/pediatric unit include the patient's general medical status, the skills and abilities of local psychiatric and general medical staffs, and the availability of suitable intensive outpatient, partial and day hospitalization, and aftercare programs to care for the patient's general medical and psychiatric problems.

2. Psychiatric management

Psychiatric management forms the foundation of treatment for patients with eating disorders and should be instituted for all patients in combination with other specific treatment modalities. Important components of psychiatric management for patients with eating disorders are as follows: establish and maintain a therapeutic alliance; coordinate care and collaborate with other clinicians; assess and monitor eating disorder symptoms and behaviors; assess and monitor the patient's general medical condition; assess and monitor the patient's psychiatric status and safety; and provide family assessment and treatment [I].

3. Choice of specific treatments for anorexia nervosa

Goals in the treatment of anorexia nervosa include restoring healthy weight (i.e., weight at which menses and ovulation in females, normal sexual drive and hormone levels in males, and normal physical and sexual growth and development in children and adolescents are restored); treating physical complications; enhancing patients' motivations to cooperate in the restoration of healthy eating patterns and to participate in treatment; providing education regarding healthy nutrition and eating patterns; correcting core maladaptive thoughts, attitudes, and feelings related to the eating disorder; treating associated psychiatric conditions, including defects in mood regulation, self-esteem, and behavior; enlisting family support and providing family counseling and therapy where appropriate; and preventing relapse.

a. Nutritional rehabilitation/counseling

A program of nutritional rehabilitation should be established for all patients who are significantly underweight [I]. Healthy target weights and expected rates of controlled weight gain (e.g., 2–3 lb/week for most inpatient and 0.5–1 lb/week for most outpatient programs) should be established. Intake levels should usually start at 30–40 kcal/kg per day (approximately 1000–1600 kcal/day) and should be advanced progressively. This may be increased to as high as 70–100 kcal/kg per day during the weight gain phase. Intake levels should be 40–60 kcal/kg per day during weight maintenance and for ongoing growth and development in children and adolescents. Patients who have higher caloric intake requirements may be discarding food, be vomiting, be exercising frequently, have increased nonexercise motor activity (e.g., fidgeting), or have truly higher metabolic rates. Vitamin and mineral supplements may also be beneficial for patients (e.g., phosphorus supplementation may be particularly useful to prevent serum hypophosphatemia).

It is essential to monitor patients medically during refeeding [I]. Monitoring should include assessment of vital signs as well as food and fluid intake and output; electrolytes (including phosphorus); and the presence of edema, rapid weight gain (associated primarily with fluid overload), congestive heart failure, and gastrointestinal symptoms, particularly constipation and bloating. Cardiac monitoring may be useful, especially at night, for children and adolescents who are severely malnourished (weight <70% of the standard body weight). Physical activity should be adapted to the food intake and energy expenditure of the patient.

Nutritional rehabilitation programs should also attempt to help patients deal with their concerns about weight gain and body image changes, educating them about the risks of their eating disorder and providing ongoing support to patients and their families [I].

b. Psychosocial interventions
The establishment and maintenance of a psychotherapeutically informed relationship is beneficial [II]. Once weight gain has started, formal psychotherapy may be very helpful. There is no clear evidence that any specific form of psychotherapy is superior for all patients. Psychosocial interventions need to be informed by understanding psychodynamic conflicts, cognitive development, psychological defenses, and complexity of family relationships as well as the presence of other psychiatric disorders. Psychotherapy alone is generally not sufficient to treat severely malnourished patients with anorexia nervosa. Ongoing treatment with individual psychotherapeutic interventions is usually required for at least a year and may take 5–6 years because of the enduring nature of many of the psychopathologic features of anorexia nervosa and the need for support during recovery.

Both the symptoms of eating disorders and problems in familial relationships that may be contributing to the maintenance of disorders may be alleviated by family and couples psychotherapy [II]. Group psychotherapy is sometimes added as an adjunctive treatment for anorexia nervosa; however, care must be taken to avoid patients competing to be the thinnest or sickest member or becoming excessively demoralized through observing the difficult, chronic course of other patients in the group.

c. Medications
Treatment of anorexia nervosa should not rely on psychotropic medications as the sole or primary treatment [I]. An assessment of the need for antidepressant medications is usually best made following weight gain, when the psychological effects of malnutrition are resolving. These medications should be considered for the prevention of relapse among weight-restored patients or to treat associated features of anorexia nervosa, such as depression or obsessive-compulsive problems [II].

4. Choice of specific treatments for bulimia nervosa

a. Nutritional rehabilitation/counseling
Nutritional counseling as an adjunct to other treatment modalities may be useful for reducing behaviors related to the eating disorder, minimizing food

restriction, increasing the variety of foods eaten, and encouraging healthy but not excessive exercise patterns [I].

b. Psychosocial interventions

A comprehensive evaluation of individual patients, their cognitive and psychological development, psychodynamic issues, cognitive style, comorbid psychopathology, patient preferences, and family situation is needed to inform the choice of psychosocial interventions [I]. Cognitive behavioral psychotherapy is the psychosocial treatment for which the most evidence for efficacy currently exists, but controlled trials have also shown interpersonal psychotherapy to be very useful. Behavioral techniques (e.g., planned meals, self-monitoring) may also be helpful. Clinical reports have indicated that psychodynamic and psychoanalytic approaches in individual or group format may be useful once bingeing and purging are improving. Patients with concurrent anorexia nervosa or severe personality disorders may benefit from extended psychotherapy.

Whenever possible, family therapy should be considered, especially for adolescents still living with parents or older patients with ongoing conflicted interactions with parents or other family members [II].

c. Medications

For most patients, antidepressant medications are effective as one component of an initial treatment [I]. Selective serotonin reuptake inhibitors (SSRIs) are currently considered to be the safest antidepressants and may be especially helpful for patients with significant symptoms of depression, anxiety, obsessions, or certain impulse disorder symptoms or for those patients who have had a suboptimal response to previous attempts at appropriate psychosocial therapy. Other antidepressant medications from a variety of classes can reduce the symptoms of binge eating and purging and may help prevent relapse among patients in remission.

While tricyclic and monoamine oxidase inhibitor (MAOI) antidepressants can be used to treat bulimia nervosa, tricyclics should be used with caution for patients who may be at high risk for suicide attempts, and MAOIs should be avoided for patients with chaotic binge eating and purging.

Emerging evidence has shown that a combination of psychotherapeutic interventions and medication results in higher remission rates and therefore should be considered when initiating treatment for patients with bulimia nervosa [II].

II. DEVELOPING A TREATMENT PLAN FOR THE INDIVIDUAL PATIENT

The following are recommendations for developing a treatment plan for individual patients with eating disorders. A number of factors should be considered when developing the treatment plan. Table 1 provides guidance for these clinical dimensions (1).

▶ A. CHOOSING A SITE OF TREATMENT

The services available for the treatment of eating disorders can range from intensive inpatient settings (in which subspecialty general medical consultation is readily available), through partial hospital and residential programs, to varying levels of outpatient care (from which the patient can receive general medical treatment, nutritional counseling, and/or individual, group, and family psychotherapy). Pretreatment evaluation of the patient is essential for determining the appropriate setting of treatment (2). Weight and cardiac and metabolic status are the most important physical parameters for determining choice of setting. Generally, patients who weigh less than approximately 85% of their individually estimated healthy weights have considerable difficulty gaining weight in the absence of a highly structured program. Those weighing less than about 75% of their individually estimated healthy weights are likely to require a 24-hour hospital program. Once weight loss is severe enough to cause the indications for immediate medical hospitalization, treatment may be less effective, refeeding may entail greater risks, and prognosis may be more problematic than when intervention is provided earlier. Knowledge about gray matter deficits that result from malnutrition and persist following refeeding also point to the need for earlier rather than later effective interventions. Therefore, hospitalization should occur before the onset of medical instability as manifested by abnormal vital signs. The decision to hospitalize should be based on psychiatric and behavioral grounds, including rapid or persistent decline in oral intake; decline in weight despite maximally intensive outpatient or partial hospitalization interventions; the presence of additional stressors—such as intercurrent viral illnesses—that may additionally interfere with the patient's ability to eat; prior knowledge of weight at which instability is likely to occur; and comorbid psychiatric problems that merit hospitalization.

Indications for immediate medical hospitalization include marked orthostatic hypotension with an increase in pulse of >20 bpm or a drop in blood pressure of >20 mm Hg/minute standing, bradycardia below 40 bpm, tachycardia over 110 bpm, or inability to sustain body core temperature (e.g., temperatures below 97.0°F). Most severely underweight patients, those with physiological instability, and many children and adolescents whose weight loss, while rapid, has not been as severe as in adult patients nonetheless require inpatient medical management and comprehensive treatment for support of weight gain. Guidelines for treatment settings are provided in table 1.

TABLE 1. Level of Care Criteria for Patients With Eating Disorders[a]

			Level of Care[b]		
Characteristic	**Level 1: Outpatient**	**Level 2: Intensive Outpatient**	**Level 3: Partial Hospitalization (Full-Day Outpatient Care)**	**Level 4: Residential Treatment Center**	**Level 5: Inpatient Hospitalization**
Medical complications	Medically stable to the extent that more extensive medical monitoring, as defined in levels 4 and 5, is not required			Medically stable to the extent that intravenous fluids, nasogastric tube feedings, or multiple daily laboratory tests are not needed	For adults: heart rate <40 bpm; blood pressure <90/60 mm Hg; glucose <60 mg/dl; potassium <3 meq/liter; electrolyte imbalance; temperature <97.0 °F; dehydration; or hepatic, renal, or cardiovascular organ compromise requiring acute treatment. For children and adolescents: heart rate in the 40s; orthostatic blood pressure changes (<20-bpm increase in heart rate or >10–20-mm Hg drop); blood pressure below 80/50 mm Hg; hypokalemia or hypophosphatemia
Suicidality	No intent or plan			Possible plan but no intent	Intent and plan
Weight as % of healthy body weight (for children, determining factor is rate of weight loss)[c]	>85%	>80%	>75%	<85%	<75% (for children and adolescents: acute weight decline with food refusal even if not <75% below healthy body weight)
Motivation to recover, including cooperativeness, insight, and ability to control obsessive thoughts	Fair to good	Fair	Partial; preoccupied with ego-syntonic thoughts more than 3 hours a day; cooperative	Poor to fair; preoccupied with ego-syntonic thoughts 4–6 hours a day; cooperative with highly structured treatment	Very poor to poor; preoccupied with ego-syntonic thoughts; uncooperative with treatment or cooperative only in highly structured environment
Comorbid disorders (substance abuse, depression, anxiety)	Presence of comorbid condition may influence choice of level of care				Any existing psychiatric disorder that would require hospitalization
Structure needed for eating/gaining weight	Self-sufficient		Needs some structure to gain weight	Needs supervision at all meals or will restrict eating	Needs supervision during and after all meals or nasogastric/special feeding

TABLE 1. Level of Care Criteria for Patients With Eating Disorders[a] *(continued)*

Characteristic	Level of Care[b]				
	Level 1: Outpatient	Level 2: Intensive Outpatient	Level 3: Partial Hospitalization (Full-Day Outpatient Care)	Level 4: Residential Treatment Center	Level 5: Inpatient Hospitalization
Impairment and ability to care for self; ability to control exercise	Able to exercise for fitness, but able to control compulsive exercising		Structure required to prevent patient from compulsive exercising	Complete role impairment, cannot eat and gain weight by self; structure required to prevent patient from compulsive exercising	
Purging behavior (laxatives and diuretics)	Can greatly reduce purging in non-structured settings; no significant medical complications such as ECG abnormalities or others suggesting the need for hospitalization			Can ask for and use support or use skills if desires to purge	Needs supervision during and after all meals and in bathrooms
Environmental stress	Others able to provide adequate emotional and practical support and structure		Others able to provide at least limited support and structure	Severe family conflict, problems, or absence so as unable to provide structured treatment in home, or lives alone without adequate support system	
Treatment availability/living situation	Lives near treatment setting			Too distant to live at home	

[a] Adapted from La Via et al. (1).

[b] One or more items in a category should qualify the patient for a higher level of care. These are not absolutes, but guidelines requiring the judgment of physicians.

[c] Although this table lists percentages of healthy body weight in relation to suggested levels of care, these are only approximations and do not correspond to percentages based on standardized tables. For any given individual, differences in body build, body composition and other physiological variables may result in considerable differences as to what constitutes a healthy body weight in relation to "norms." For some, a healthy body weight may be 110% of "standard," whereas for others it may be 98%. Each individual's physiological differences must be assessed and appreciated.

Although most patients with uncomplicated bulimia nervosa do not require hospitalization, indications for hospitalization can include severe disabling symptoms that have not responded to adequate trials of competent outpatient treatment, serious concurrent general medical problems (e.g., metabolic abnormalities, hematemesis, vital sign changes, or the appearance of uncontrolled vomiting), suicidality, psychiatric disturbances that would warrant the patient's hospitalization independent of the eating disorders diagnosis, or severe concurrent alcohol or drug abuse.

Legal interventions, including involuntary hospitalization and legal guardianship, may be necessary to ensure the safety of treatment-reluctant patients whose general medical conditions are life-threatening (3). Decisions to hospitalize on a psychiatric versus general medical or adolescent/pediatric unit depend on the patient's general medical status, the skills and abilities of local psychiatric and general medical staffs, and the availability of suitable programs to care for the patient's general medical and psychiatric problems (4). Some evidence suggests that patients treated in eating disorders inpatient specialty units have better outcomes than patients treated in general inpatient settings that lack expertise and experience in treating patients with eating disorders (5).

Partial hospitalization and day hospital programs are being increasingly used in attempts to decrease the length of some inpatient hospitalizations; for milder cases, these programs are being increasingly used in place of hospitalization. However, such programs may not be appropriate for patients with lower initial weights (e.g., those who are ≤75% of average weight for height). In clinical practice, failure of outpatient treatment is one of the most frequent indications for more intensive treatment, either day/partial hospital or inpatient. In deciding whether to treat in a partial hospitalization program, the patient's level of motivation to participate in treatment and ability to work in a group setting should be considered (6, 7).

Patients with high motivation to comply with treatment, cooperative families, brief symptom duration, and who are less than 20% below healthy body weight may benefit from treatment in outpatient settings, but only if they are carefully monitored and if they and their families understand that a more restrictive setting may be necessary if persistent progress is not evident in a few weeks (8–10). Careful monitoring includes at least weekly (and often two to three times a week) postvoiding gowned weighings, which may also include measurement of urine specific gravity together with orthostatic vital signs and temperatures. While patients treated in the outpatient setting can remain with their families and continue to attend school or work, these advantages must be balanced against the risks of failure to progress in recovery.

▶ B. PSYCHIATRIC MANAGEMENT

Psychiatric management includes a broad range of tasks that are performed by the psychiatrist or that the psychiatrist should ensure are provided to the patient with an eating disorder. These should be instituted for all patients with eating disorders in combination with other specific treatment modalities.

1. Establish and maintain a therapeutic alliance

At the very outset, clinicians should attempt to build trust, establish mutual respect, and develop a therapeutic relationship with the patient that will serve as the basis for ongoing exploration and treatment of the problems associated with the eating disorder. Eating disorders are frequently long-term illnesses that can manifest themselves in different ways at different points during their course; treating them often requires the psychiatrist to adapt and modify therapeutic strategies over time. During the course of treatment, patients with eating disorders may resist looking beyond immediate eating disorder symptoms to comorbid psychopathology and underlying psychodynamics. Psychiatrists should be mindful of the fact that the interventions they prescribe for individuals with anorexia nervosa create extreme anxieties in the patients. Encouraging them to gain weight asks for them to do the very thing of which they are most frightened. Recognizing and acknowledging to patients one's awareness of these effects can assist in building the therapeutic alliance and decrease the patients' perceptions that the psychiatrist just wants to make them fat and does not understand or empathize with their underlying emotions. Addressing these resistances may be important in allowing treatment to proceed through impasses as well as helping to ameliorate factors that serve to aggravate and maintain eating disorders (11).

Patients with eating disorders also present treating physicians with extraordinary challenges in understanding and working with countertransference reactions. Because these illnesses are often difficult to ameliorate with short-term interventions, they often evoke the feeling in treating clinicians that they have not done enough to change or alleviate the patient's plight. A frequent range of countertransference feelings include beleaguerment, demoralization, and excessive needs to change the patient with a chronic eating disorder. Some authorities have observed that the gender of the therapist plays a role in the particular kind of countertransference reactions that come into play (12–14). Concerns about choice of gender of the therapist may be tied to patient concerns about boundary violations and should be attended to in selecting health care providers (15, 16). In addition to gender differences, cultural differences between patients and therapists and between patients and other aspects of the care system may also influence the course and conduct of treatment and require mindful attention. Most authorities believe ongoing processing of one's countertransference reactions, sometimes with the help of a supervisor or consultant, can be useful in helping the therapist persevere and reconcile intense, troublesome countertransference reactions. Regardless of the theoretical base the clinician uses, countertransference reactions have been described by a wide variety of therapists who used differing clinical approaches (13, 14, 17–22).

Patients who have been sexually abused or who have otherwise been the victims of boundary violations are prone to stir a profound need to rescue the patient, which can occasionally result in a loosening of the therapeutic structure, loss of therapeutic boundary keeping, and a sexualized countertransference reaction. In some cases, these countertransference responses have led to overt sexual acting out and unethical treatment on the part of the therapist, which may not only compromise treatment but also severely harm the patient (23). Clear boundaries are critical in the treatment of all patients with eating disorders, not only those who have been sexually abused but also those who may have experienced other types of boundary intrusions regarding their bodies, eating behaviors, and other aspects of the self by family members and others.

2. Coordinate care and collaborate with other clinicians

An important task for the psychiatrist is to coordinate and, depending on expertise, oversee the care of patients with eating disorders. A variety of professionals may collaborate in the care and provide such services as nutritional counseling, working with the family, and establishing various individual and group psychotherapeutic, cognitive behavior, or behavior programs. Other physician specialists and dentists should be consulted when necessary for management of general medical (e.g., cardiac dysfunction) and dental complications. Particularly in treatment settings where the staff does not have training or experience dealing with patients with eating disorders, the provision of education and supervision by the psychiatrist can be crucial to the success of treatment (24).

3. Assess and monitor eating disorder symptoms and behaviors

The psychiatrist should make a careful assessment of the patient's eating disorder symptoms and behaviors (25). Obtaining a detailed report of a single day or using a calendar as a prompt may help elicit specific information, particularly regarding perceived intake. Having a meal together or observing a meal may provide useful information, permitting the clinician to observe difficulties patients may have in eating particular foods, anxieties that erupt in the course of a meal, and rituals concerning food (such as cutting, separating, or mashing) that they may feel compelled to perform. The patient's understanding of how the illness developed and the effects of any interpersonal problems on the onset of the eating disorder should be explored. Family history should be obtained regarding eating disorders and other psychiatric disorders, obesity, family interactions in relation to the patient's disorder, and attitudes toward eating, exercise, and appearance. It is essential not to articulate theory in order to blame or permit family members to blame one another or themselves. Rather, the point is to identify stressors whose amelioration may facilitate recovery. In the assessment of young patients, it may be helpful to involve parents, school personnel, and health professionals who routinely work with children. The complete assessment usually requires at least several hours, and often patients and their families may not initially reveal pertinent information about sensitive issues, even when directly questioned. Some important information may be uncovered only after a trusting relationship has been established and the patient is better able to accurately identify inner emotional states.

Formal measures are also available for the assessment of eating disorders, including self-report questionnaires and semistructured interviews. Representative examples are listed in table 2.

TABLE 2. Representative Instruments for Assessment of Eating Disorders

Instrument	Form of Administration	Comments	Reference(s)
Diagnostic Survey for Eating Disorders (DSED)	Can be used as self-report or semistructured interview	Twelve sections cover demographics, weight history and body image, dieting, binge eating, purging, exercise, related behaviors, sexual functioning, menstruation, medical and psychiatric history, life adjustment, and family history	Johnson C: Diagnostic Survey for Eating Disorders (DSED), in The Etiology and Treatment of Bulimia Nervosa. Edited by Johnson C, Connors M. New York, Basic Books, 1987
Eating Attitudes Test	Self-report	Brief (26-item), standardized, self-report screening test of symptoms and concerns characteristic of eating disorders; completion time: 5–10 minutes	Garner DM, Olmsted MP, Bohr Y, Garfinkel PE: The Eating Attitudes Test: psychometric features and clinical correlates. Psychol Med 1982; 12:871–878

Garner DM: Psychoeducational principles in the treatment of eating disorders, in Handbook for Treatment of Eating Disorders. Edited by Garner DM, Garfinkel PE. New York, Guilford Press, 1997, pp 145–177 |
| Eating Disorders Examination (EDE) | Semistructured interview | Measures the presence and severity of eating disorder features and provides operational DSM-IV diagnoses | Fairburn CG, Cooper Z: The Eating Disorders Examination—12th ed, in Binge Eating: Nature, Assessment and Treatment. Edited by Fairburn CG, Wilson GT. New York, Guilford Press, 1993 |
| EDE-Q4 | Self-report | Self-report version of the EDE, designed for situations in which an interview cannot be used; validated against the EDE | Fairburn CG, Beglin SJ: The assessment of eating disorders: interview or self-report questionnaire? Int J Eat Disord 1994; 16:363–370 |

TABLE 2. Representative Instruments for Assessment of Eating Disorders *(continued)*

Instrument	Form of Administration	Comments	Reference(s)
Eating Disorders Inventory	Self-report	Standardized measure of psychological traits and symptom clusters presumed to have relevance to understanding and treatment of eating disorders; 11 subscales presented in 6-point, forced choice format; three scales assess attitudes and behaviors concerning eating, weight, and shape; eight more scales assess more general psychological traits; completion time: 20 minutes	Garner DM, Olmstead MJ, Polivy J: Development and validation of a multidimensional eating disorder inventory for anorexia nervosa and bulimia. Int J Eat Disord 1983; 2:15–34 Garner DM: The Eating Disorders Inventory—2 Professional Manual. Odessa, Fla, Psychological Assessment Resources, 1991 Garner DM: The Eating Disorders Inventory—2 (EDI-2), in Outcomes Assessments in Clinical Practice. Edited by Sederer LI, Dickey B. Baltimore, Williams & Wilkins, 1996, pp 92–96
Eating Disorders Questionnaire	Self-report	Questions address eating disorders symptoms, associated symptoms, time course, treatment	Mitchell JE, Hatsukami D, Eckert E, Pyle RL: The Eating Disorders Questionnaire. Psychopharmacol Bull 1985; 21:1025–1043
Questionnaire of Eating and Weight Patterns	Self-report	Measures the nature and quantity of binge eating to assess binge-eating disorder	Yanovski SZ: Binge eating disorder: current knowledge and future directions. Obesity Res 1993; 1:306–320 Nangle DW, Ghonson WG, Carr-Nangle RD, Engler LB: Binge eating disorder and the proposed DSM-IV criteria: psychometric analysis of the Questionnaire of Eating and Weight Patterns. Int J Eat Disord 1993; 16:147–157
Yale-Brown-Cornell Eating Disorder Scale	Clinical conducted interview	Includes a 65-item symptom checklist plus 19 questions, covering 18 general categories of rituals and preoccupations; requires 15 minutes or less to complete	Mazure CM, Halmi KA, Sunday SR, Romano SJ, Einhorn AN: Yale-Brown-Cornell Eating Disorder Scale: development, use, reliability and validity. J Psychiatr Res 1994; 28:425–445 Sunday SR, Halmi KA, Einhorn AN: The Yale-Brown-Cornell Eating Disorder Scale: a new scale to assess eating disorders symptomatology. Int J Eat Disord 1995; 18:237–245

4. Assess and monitor the patient's general medical condition

A full physical examination should be performed by a physician familiar with common findings in patients with eating disorders, with particular attention to vital signs; physical and sexual growth and development (including height and weight); the cardiovascular system; and evidence of dehydration, acrocyanosis, lanugo, salivary gland enlargement, and scarring on the dorsum of the hands (Russell's sign). A dental examination should also be performed. It is generally useful to assess growth, sexual development, and general physical development in younger patients. The use of a pediatric growth chart may permit identification of patients who have failed to gain weight and who have growth retardation (26).

The need for laboratory analyses should be determined on an individual basis depending on the patient's condition or when necessary for making treatment decisions. Some laboratory assessments indicated for patients with eating disorders and for specific clinical features appear in table 3.

TABLE 3. Laboratory Assessments for Patients With Eating Disorders

Assessment	Patient Indication
Basic analyses	Consider for all patients with eating disorders
Blood chemistry studies	
Serum electrolyte level	
Blood urea nitrogen (BUN) level	
Creatinine level	
Thyroid function test	
Complete blood count (CBC)	
Urinalysis	
Additional analyses	Consider for malnourished and severely symptomatic patients
Blood chemistry studies	
Calcium level	
Magnesium level	
Phosphorus level	
Liver function tests	
Electrocardiogram	
Osteopenia and osteoporosis assessments	Consider for patients underweight more than 6 months
Dual-energy X-ray absorptiometry (DEXA)	
Estradiol level	
Testosterone level in males	
Nonroutine assessments	Consider only for specific unusual indications
Serum amylase level	Possible indicator of persistent or recurrent vomiting
Luteinizing hormone (LH) and follicle-stimulating hormone (FSH) levels	For persistent amenorrhea at normal weight
Brain magnetic resonance imaging (MRI) and computerized tomography (CT)	For ventricular enlargement correlated with degree of malnutrition
Stool	For blood

5. Assess and monitor the patient's psychiatric status and safety

Attention should be paid to comorbid psychiatric disturbances, especially affective and anxiety disorders, suicidality, substance abuse, obsessive and compulsive symptoms, and personality disturbances. Shoplifting, stealing food, and self-mutilatory behaviors should be noted. A developmental history should attend to temperament, psychological, sexual and physical abuse, and sexual history. Psychological testing, particularly after nutritional rehabilitation, may clarify personality and neuropsychological disturbances. In addition to assessing behavioral and formal psychopathological aspects of the case, it is always useful to investigate psychodynamic and interpersonal conflicts that may be relevant to understanding and treating the patient's eating disorder.

6. Provide family assessment and treatment

Eating disorders impose substantial burdens on the families of patients. Parents often avoid recognizing that the child or adolescent is ill and may have difficulties in accepting the seriousness of the illness. Parents then often struggle with the belief that they have themselves caused the illness and need help overcoming their guilt so that they can face their children's needs. The feelings of guilt are exacerbated by the rejection of their parenting that is implicit in the child's refusal of nurturance in the form of food. Parents also have difficulties in accepting the need for treatment or requiring that their child accept treatment, since the child's protest that treatment is noxious only increases the parent's guilt. Parents typically become angry at their child's secretive purging, exercising, and other efforts to avoid food or burn off calories and may come to view the children as "manipulative" rather than desperate. Parents may increasingly avoid their responsibilities of providing meals within specific contexts that bind family relationships. They are often riddled with anxieties that their child will die and, depending on the family and gravity of the case, may go on to develop anger, exhaustion, and despair. The patient's and family's preoccupations, social concerns, and rituals may begin to orient and focus around the illness, particularly family interactions involving meals. Decisions concerning food may impact family get-togethers, social visits, vacations, and even vocational choices.

Assessment of the family is important whenever possible, particularly for patients living at home or those who are enmeshed with their families. Family assessment may be extremely useful for some patients in order to understand interactions that may contribute to ongoing illness or that may potentially facilitate recovery. Comprehensive treatment of the patient should include an assessment of the burden of the illness on the family, with support and education given to the family as part of the overall treatment.

▶ C. CHOICE OF SPECIFIC TREATMENTS FOR ANOREXIA NERVOSA

The aims of treatment are to 1) restore patients to healthy weight (at which menses and normal ovulation in females, normal sexual drive and hormone levels in males, and normal physical and sexual growth and development in children and adolescents are restored); 2) treat physical complications; 3) enhance patients' motivations to cooperate in the restoration of healthy eating patterns and to participate in treatment; 4) provide education regarding healthy nutrition and eating patterns; 5) correct core dysfunctional thoughts, attitudes, and feelings related to the eating disorder; 6) treat associated psychiatric conditions, including defects in mood regulation, self-esteem, and behavior; 7) enlist family support and provide family counseling and therapy where appropriate; and 8) prevent relapse.

1. Nutritional rehabilitation

For patients who are markedly underweight, a program of nutritional rehabilitation should be established. Hospital-based programs should be considered, particularly for the most nutritionally compromised patients (e.g., those whose weight is less than 75% of the recommended weight for their height or for children and adolescents whose weight loss may not be as severe but who are losing weight at a rapid rate). Nutritional rehabilitation programs should establish healthy target weights and have expected rates of controlled weight gain (e.g., 2–3 lb/week for inpatient units and 0.5–1 lb/week for outpatient programs). Intake levels should usually start at 30–40 kcal/kg per day (approximately 1000–1600 kcal/day) and should be advanced progressively. During the weight gain phase, intake may be increased to as high as 70–100 kcal/kg per day for some patients. During weight maintenance and for ongoing growth and development in children and adolescents, intake levels should be 40–60 kcal/kg per day. Patients who require higher caloric intakes may be discarding food, vomiting, or exercising frequently or have more nonexercise motor activity such as fidgeting; others may have a truly elevated metabolic rate. In addition to calories, patients benefit from vitamin and mineral supplements (and in particular may require phosphorus before serum hypophosphatemia occurs). Medical monitoring during refeeding is essential and should include assessment of vital signs as well as food and fluid intake and output; monitoring of electrolytes (including phosphorus); and observation for edema, rapid weight gain associated primarily with fluid overload, congestive heart failure, and gastrointestinal symptoms, particularly constipation and bloating. For children and adolescents who are severely malnourished (weight <70% standard body weight) cardiac monitoring, especially at night, may be desirable. Physical activity should be adapted to the food intake and energy expenditure of the patient.

Other treatment options for nutritional rehabilitation include temporary supplementation or replacement of regular food with liquid food supplements. On occasion, nasogastric feedings may be required. In life-threatening or very unusual circumstances, parenteral feedings for brief periods may be considered; however, infection is always a risk with parenteral feedings in emaciated and potentially immunocompromised patients with anorexia nervosa. These forceful interventions should be considered only when patients are unwilling to cooperate with oral feedings; when the patient's health, physical safety, and recovery are being threatened; and after appropriate legal and ethical considerations have been taken into account.

Additional goals of nutritional rehabilitation programs include education, ongoing support, and helping patients deal with their concerns about weight gain and body image changes.

2. Psychosocial interventions

It is essential that psychosocial interventions incorporate an understanding of psychodynamic conflicts, cognitive development, psychological defenses, and the complexity of family relationships as well as the presence of other psychiatric disorders. Although research studies regarding psychotherapy treat different interventions as distinctly separate treatments, in practice there is frequent overlap. Most nutritional rehabilitation programs employ a milieu incorporating emotional nurturance and one of a variety of behavioral interventions (which involve a combination of reinforcers that link exercise, bed rest, and privileges to target weights, desired behaviors, and informational feedback). Other forms of individual psychotherapy are also used in the treatment of anorexia nervosa, initiated as the patient is gaining weight. However, there has been little formal study of the optimal role for either individual or group psychotherapy in treating anorexia nervosa. Because of the enduring nature of many of the psychopathologic features of anorexia nervosa and the need for support during recovery, ongoing treatment with individual psychotherapeutic interventions is frequently required for at least a year and may take 5–6 years (27).

Family therapy and couples psychotherapy are frequently useful for both symptom alleviation and alleviation of problems in familial relationships that may be contributing to the maintenance of the disorders. Some practitioners use group psychotherapy as an adjunctive treatment for anorexia nervosa, but caution must be taken that patients do not compete to be the thinnest or sickest patient or become excessively demoralized through bearing witness to the difficult, ongoing struggles of other patients in the group.

Programs that focus exclusively on the need for abstinence (e.g., 12-step programs) without attending to nutritional considerations or cognitive and behavioral deficits are not recommended as the sole initial treatment approach for anorexia nervosa; interventions based on addiction models blended with features of other psychotherapeutic approaches can be considered. Support groups led by professionals or advocacy organizations may be beneficial as adjuncts to other psychosocial treatment modalities.

3. Medications

Psychotropic medications should not be used as the sole or primary treatment for anorexia nervosa. In addition, medication therapy should not be used routinely during the weight restoration period. The role for antidepressants is usually best assessed following weight gain, when the psychological effects of malnutrition are resolving. However, these medications should be considered to prevent relapse among weight-restored patients or to treat associated features of anorexia nervosa, such as depression or obsessive-compulsive problems.

▶ D. CHOICE OF SPECIFIC TREATMENTS FOR BULIMIA NERVOSA

1. Nutritional rehabilitation/counseling

A primary focus for nutritional rehabilitation concerns monitoring the patient's patterns of binge eating and purging. Most patients with bulimia nervosa are of normal weight, so nutritional restoration will not be a central focus of treatment. However, even among patients of normal weight, nutritional counseling as an adjunct to other treatment modalities may be useful for reducing behaviors related to the eating disorder, minimizing food restriction, increasing the variety of foods eaten, and encouraging healthy but not excessive exercise patterns.

2. Psychosocial interventions

Psychosocial interventions should be chosen on the basis of a comprehensive evaluation of the individual patient, considering cognitive and psychological development, psychodynamic issues, cognitive style, comorbid psychopathology, patient preferences, and family situation. With respect to short-term interventions for treating acute episodes of bulimia nervosa, cognitive behavioral psychotherapy is the psychosocial treatment for which the most evidence for efficacy currently exists. However, controlled trials have also shown interpersonal psychotherapy to be very useful for this disorder. Behavioral techniques, such as planned meals and self-monitoring, may also be helpful for initial symptom management and interrupting the binge-purge behaviors. There are clinical reports indicating that psychodynamic and psychoanalytic approaches in individual or group format are useful once bingeing and purging are improving. These approaches address developmental issues, identity formation, body image concerns, sexual and aggressive difficulties, affect regulation, gender role expectations, interpersonal conflicts, family dysfunction, coping styles, and problem solving. Some patients, such as those with concurrent anorexia nervosa or concurrent severe personality disorders, may benefit from extended psychotherapy.

Family therapy should be considered whenever possible, especially for adolescents still living with parents or older patients with ongoing conflicted interactions with parents. Patients with marital discord may benefit from couples therapy. Support groups and 12-step programs such as Overeaters Anonymous may be helpful as adjuncts to initial treatment of bulimia nervosa and for subsequent relapse prevention but are not recommended as the sole initial treatment approach for bulimia nervosa.

3. Medications

Antidepressants are effective as one component of an initial treatment program for most patients. Although antidepressant medications from a variety of classes can reduce symptoms of binge eating and purging and may help prevent relapse among patients in remission, SSRIs are safest. They may be especially helpful for patients with substantial symptoms of depression, anxiety, obsessions, or certain impulse disorder symptoms, or for patients who have failed or had a suboptimal response to previous attempts at appropriate psychosocial therapy. Dose levels of tricyclic and MAOI antidepressants for treating bulimia nervosa are similar to those used to treat depression; practitioners should try to avoid prescribing tricyclics to patients who may be suicidal and MAOIs to patients with chaotic binge eating and purging.

4. Combinations of psychosocial interventions and medications
In some research, the combination of antidepressant therapy and cognitive behavioral therapy results in the highest remission rates. Therefore, clinicians should consider a combination of psychotherapeutic interventions and medication when initiating treatment.

III. DISEASE DEFINITION, EPIDEMIOLOGY, AND NATURAL HISTORY

▶ ## A. CLINICAL FEATURES

The DSM-IV criteria for establishing the diagnosis of anorexia nervosa or bulimia nervosa appear in table 4 and table 5, respectively.

Although DSM-IV criteria allow clinicians to diagnose patients with a specific eating disorder, the symptoms frequently occur along a continuum between those of anorexia nervosa and those of bulimia nervosa. Weight preoccupation and excessive self-evaluation of weight and shape are primary symptoms in both anorexia nervosa and bulimia nervosa, and many patients demonstrate a mixture of both anorexic and bulimic behaviors. For example, up to 50% of patients with anorexia nervosa develop bulimic symptoms, and some patients who are initially bulimic develop anorexic symptoms (28). Atypical patients—who deny fear of weight gain, appraise their bodies as malnourished, and deny distorted perceptions of their bodies—are not uncommon among Asian patients (29). In one U.S. series (30), these atypical features were seen in about one-fifth of the patients admitted to a specialty eating disorder program.

Anorexia nervosa appears in two subtypes: restricting and binge-eating/purging; classification into subtypes is based on the presence of bulimic symptoms. Patients with anorexia nervosa can alternate between bulimic and restricting subtypes at different periods of their illness (31–36). Among the binge-eating/purging subtype of patients with anorexia nervosa, further distinctions can be made between those who both binge and purge and those who purge but do not objectively binge. Patients with bulimia nervosa can be subclassified into the purging subtype and the nonpurging subtype. Many patients, particularly in younger age groups, have combinations of eating disorder symptoms that cannot be strictly categorized as either anorexia nervosa or bulimia nervosa and are technically diagnosed as "eating disorder not otherwise specified" (37).

Patients with anorexia nervosa and bulimia nervosa often experience other associated psychiatric symptoms and behaviors. Individuals with anorexia nervosa often demonstrate social isolation. Depressive, anxious, and obsessional symptoms, perfectionistic traits, and rigid cognitive styles as well as sexual disinterest are often present among restricting anorexic patients (38). Early in the course of illness, patients with anorexia nervosa often have limited recognition of their disorder and experience their symptoms as ego-syntonic; this is sometimes accompanied by corresponding limited recognition by the family. Depressive, anxious, and impulsive symptoms as well as sexual conflicts and disturbances with intimacy are often associated with bulimia nervosa. Although patients with bulimia nervosa are likely to recognize their disorder, shame frequently prevents them from seeking treatment at an early stage (39–42). Patients with anorexia nervosa of the binge-eating/purging subtype are

TABLE 4. DSM-IV Criteria for Anorexia Nervosa

Criterion	Description
A	Refusal to maintain body weight at or above a minimally normal weight for age and height (e.g., weight loss leading to maintenance of body weight less than 85% of that expected or failure to make expected weight gain during period of growth, leading to body weight less than 85% of that expected).
B	Intense fear of gaining weight or becoming fat, even though underweight.
C	Disturbance in the way in which one's body weight or shape is experienced, undue influence of body weight or shape on self-evaluation, or denial of the seriousness of the current low body weight.
D	In postmenarcheal females, amenorrhea, i.e., the absence of at least three consecutive menstrual cycles. (A woman is considered to have amenorrhea if her periods occur only following hormone, e.g., estrogen, administration.)
Specify type	
Restricting type	During the current episode of anorexia nervosa, the person has not regularly engaged in binge-eating or purging behavior (i.e., self-induced vomiting or the misuse of laxatives, diuretics, or enemas).
Binge-eating/purging type	During the current episode of anorexia nervosa, the person has regularly engaged in a binge-eating or purging behavior (i.e., self-induced vomiting or the misuse of laxatives, diuretics, or enemas).

sometimes suicidal and self-harming. In one subgroup of patients with bulimia nervosa (the "multi-impulsive" bulimic patients), significant degrees of impulsivity (manifested as stealing, self-harm behaviors, suicidality, substance abuse, and sexual promiscuity) have been observed (43).

Some of the clinical features associated with eating disorders may result from malnutrition or semistarvation (44, 45). Studies of volunteers who have submitted to semistarvation and semistarved prisoners of war report the development of food preoccupation, food hoarding, abnormal taste preferences, binge eating, and other disturbances of appetite regulation as well as symptoms of depression, obsessionality, apathy, irritability, and other personality changes. In patients with anorexia nervosa, some of these starvation-related state phenomena, such as abnormal taste preference, may completely reverse with refeeding, although it may take considerable time after weight restoration for them to abate completely (46). However, some of these symptoms may reflect both preexisting and enduring traits, such as obsessive-compulsiveness, which are then further exacerbated by semistarvation and, therefore, may only be partially reversed with nutritional rehabilitation (47). Complete psychological assessments may not be possible until some degree of weight normalization is achieved (48). Although patients with bulimia nervosa may appear to be physically within the standards of healthy weight, they may also show psychological and biological correlates of semistarvation—such as depression, irritability, and obsessionality—and may be below a biologically

TABLE 5. DSM-IV Criteria for Bulimia Nervosa

Criterion	Description
A	Recurrent episodes of binge eating. An episode of binge eating is characterized by both of the following: (1) Eating, in a discrete period of time (e.g., within any 2-hour period), an amount of food that is definitely larger than most people would eat during a similar period of time and under similar circumstances. (2) A sense of lack of control over eating during the episode (e.g., a feeling that one cannot stop eating or control what or how much one is eating).
B	Recurrent inappropriate compensatory behavior in order to prevent weight gain, such as self-induced vomiting; misuse of laxatives, diuretics, enemas, or other medications; fasting; or excessive exercise.
C	The binge eating and inappropriate compensatory behaviors both occur, on average, at least twice a week for 3 months.
D	Self-evaluation is unduly influenced by body shape and weight.
E	The disturbance does not occur exclusively during episodes of anorexia nervosa.
Specify type	
Purging type	During the current episode of bulimia nervosa, the person has regularly engaged in self-induced vomiting or the misuse of laxatives, diuretics, or enemas.
Nonpurging type	During the current episode of bulimia nervosa, the person has used other inappropriate compensatory behaviors, such as fasting or excessive exercise, but has not regularly engaged in self-induced vomiting or the misuse of laxatives, diuretics, or enemas.

determined set-point even at a weight considered to be "normal" according to population norms (49, 50).

Common physical complications of anorexia nervosa are listed in table 6. Amenorrhea of even a few months may be associated with osteopenia, which may progress to potentially irreversible osteoporosis and a correspondingly higher rate of pathological fractures (51–53). Pains in the extremities may signal stress fractures that may not be evident from examination of plain X-rays but whose presence may be signaled by abnormal bone scan results. Patients with anorexia nervosa who develop hypoestrogenemic amenorrhea in their teenage years that persists into young adulthood are at greatest risk for osteoporosis, since they not only lose bone mass but also fail to form bone at a critical phase of development. As a result, prepubertal and early pubertal patients are also at risk of permanent growth stunting (54). The areas most vulnerable to osteoporosis are the lumbar spine and hip.

Acute complications of anorexia nervosa include dehydration, electrolyte disturbances (with purging), cardiac compromise with various arrhythmias (including conduction defects and ventricular arrhythmias), gastrointestinal motility disturbances, renal problems, infertility, premature births, other perinatal complications, hypothermia, and other evidence of hypometabolism (55). Death from anorexia nervosa is often proximally due to cardiac arrest secondary to arrhythmias.

TABLE 6. Physical Complications of Anorexia Nervosa

Organ System	Symptoms	Signs	Laboratory Test Results
Whole body	Weakness, lassitude	Malnutrition	Low weight/body mass index, low body fat percentage per anthropometrics or underwater weighing
Central nervous system	Apathy, poor concentration	Cognitive impairment; depressed, irritable mood	CT scan: ventricular enlargement; MRI: decreased gray and white matter
Cardiovascular and peripheral vascular	Palpitations, weakness, dizziness, shortness of breath, chest pain, coldness of extremities	Irregular, weak, slow pulse; marked orthostatic blood pressure changes; peripheral vasoconstriction with acrocyanosis	ECG: bradycardia, arrhythmias; Q-Tc prolongation (dangerous sign)
Skeletal	Bone pain with exercise	Point tenderness; short stature/arrested skeletal growth	X-rays or bone scan for pathological stress fractures; bone densitometry for bone mineral density assessment for osteopenia or osteoporosis
Muscular	Weakness, muscle aches	Muscle wasting	Muscle enzyme abnormalities in severe malnutrition
Reproductive	Arrested psychosexual maturation or interest; loss of libido	Loss of menses or primary amenorrhea; arrested sexual development or regression of secondary sex characteristics; fertility problems; higher rates of pregnancy and neonatal complications	Hypoestrogenemia; prepubertal patterns of LH, FSH secretion; lack of follicular development/dominant follicle on pelvic ultrasound
Endocrine, metabolic	Fatigue; cold intolerance; diuresis; vomiting	Low body temperature (hypothermia)	Elevated serum cortisol; increase in rT3 ("reverse" T3); dehydration; electrolyte abnormalities; hypophosphatemia (especially on refeeding); hypoglycemia (rare)
Hematologic	Fatigue; cold intolerance	Rare bruising/clotting abnormalities	Anemia; neutropenia with relative lymphocytosis; thrombocytopenia; low erythrocyte sedimentation rate; rarely clotting factor abnormalities
Gastrointestinal	Vomiting; abdominal pain; bloating; obstipation; constipation	Abdominal distension with meals; abnormal bowel sounds	Delayed gastric emptying; occasionally abnormal liver function test results
Genitourinary		Pitting edema	Elevated BUN; low glomerular filtration rate; greater formation of renal calculi; hypovolemic nephropathy
Integument	Change in hair	Lanugo	

Common physical complications of bulimic behaviors are listed in table 7. The most serious physical complications occur in patients with chronic and severe patterns of binge eating and purging and are most concerning in very-low-weight patients (56).

Laboratory abnormalities in anorexia nervosa may include neutropenia with relative lymphocytosis, abnormal liver function, hypoglycemia, hypercortisolemia, hypercholesterolemia, hypercarotenemia, low serum zinc levels, electrolyte disturbances, and widespread disturbances in endocrine function. Thyroid abnormalities may include low T_3 and T_4 levels, which are reversible with weight restoration and generally should not be treated with replacement therapy (57–60). Normal serum phosphorus values may be misleading, since they do not reflect total body phosphorus depletion (which is usually reflected in serum phosphorus only after refeeding has begun). In very severe cases of malnutrition, elevated serum levels of muscle enzymes associated with catabolism may be seen in more than one-half of the patients with anorexia nervosa (61).

MRI abnormalities reflect changes in the brain. White matter and cerebrospinal fluid volumes appear to return to the normal range following weight restoration. However, gray matter volume deficits, which correlate with the patient's lowest recorded body mass indices, may persist even after weight restoration (62–66). Some patients show persistent deficits in their neuropsychological testing results, which has been shown to be associated with poorer outcomes (67).

It is important to consider that laboratory findings in anorexia nervosa may be normal in spite of profound malnutrition. For example, patients may have low total body potassium levels even when serum electrolytes are normal and thus may be prone to unpredictable cardiac arrhythmias (68).

Laboratory abnormalities in bulimia nervosa may include electrolyte imbalances such as hypokalemia, hypochloremic alkalosis, mild elevations of serum amylase, and hypomagnesemia and hypophosphatemia, especially in laxative abusers (57, 69).

▶ B. NATURAL HISTORY AND COURSE

1. Anorexia nervosa

The percentage of individuals with anorexia nervosa who *fully* recover is modest. Although some patients improve symptomatically over time, a substantial proportion continue to have disturbances with body image, disordered eating, and other psychiatric difficulties (70). A review of a large number of carefully done follow-up studies conducted with hospitalized or tertiary referral populations at least 4 years after onset of illness show that the outcomes of about 44% of the patients could be rated as good (weight restored to within 15% of recommended weight for height; regular menstruation established), about 24% were poor (weight never reached within 15% of recommended weight for height; menstruation absent or at best sporadic), and about 28% of the outcomes fell between those of the good and poor groups; approximately 5% of the patients had died (early mortality). Overall, about two-thirds

TABLE 7. Physical Complications of Bulimia Nervosa

Organ System	Symptoms	Signs	Laboratory Test Results
Metabolic	Weakness; irritability	Poor skin turgor	Dehydration (urine specific gravity; osmolality); serum electrolytes: hypokalemic, hypochloremic alkalosis in those who vomit; hypomagnesemia and hypophosphatemia in laxative abusers
Gastrointestinal	Abdominal pain and discomfort in vomiters; occasionally automatic vomiting; obstipation; constipation; bowel irregularities and bloating in laxative abusers	Occasionally blood-streaked vomitus; vomiters may occasionally have gastritis, esophagitis, gastroesophageal erosions, esophageal dysmotility patterns (including gastroesophageal reflux, and, very rarely, Mallory-Weiss [esophageal] or gastric tears); may have increased rates of pancreatitis; chronic laxative abusers may show colonic dysmotility or melanosis coli	
Reproductive	Fertility problems	Spotty/scanty menstrual periods	May be hypoestrogenemic
Oropharyngeal	Dental decay; pain in pharynx; swollen cheeks and neck (painless)	Dental caries with erosion of dental enamel, particularly lingular surface of incisors; erythema of pharynx; enlarged salivary glands	X-rays confirm erosion of dental enamel; elevated serum amylase associated with benign parotid hyperplasia
Integument		Scarring on dorsum of hand (Russell's sign)	
Cardiomuscular (in ipecac abusers)	Weakness; palpitations	Cardiac abnormalities; muscle weakness	Cardiomyopathy and peripheral myopathy

of patients continue to have enduring morbid food and weight preoccupation, and up to 40% have bulimic symptoms. Even among those who have goods outcomes as defined by restoration of weight and menses, many have other persistent psychiatric symptoms, including dysthymia, social phobia, obsessive-compulsive symptoms, and substance abuse (71). In a carefully done 10–15-year follow-up study of adolescent patients hospitalized for anorexia nervosa—76% of whom met criteria for full recovery—time to recovery was quite protracted, ranging from 57 to 79 months depending on the definition of recovery (27, 30). Anorexic patients with atypical features, such as denying either a fear of gaining weight or a distorted perception of their bodies, had a somewhat better course (30). Mortality, which primarily resulted from cardiac arrest or suicide, has been found to increase with length of follow-up, reaching up to 20% among patients followed for more than 20 years (72). A 1995 meta-analysis suggests a 5.6% mortality rate per decade (73). However, in the aforementioned 10–15-year follow-up study of adolescents, in which patients received intensive treatment, no deaths were reported (27). Some studies estimate that death rates of young women with anorexia nervosa are up to 12 times those of age-matched women in the community and up to twice those of women with any other psychiatric disorders. However, these studies have involved clinical populations, and it is not clear what the corresponding community rates would be (73). Nevertheless, recent data suggest that of all psychiatric disorders, the greatest excess of patient mortality due to natural and unnatural causes is associated with eating disorders and substance abuse (74).

Poorer prognosis has been associated with initial lower minimum weight, the presence of vomiting, failure to respond to previous treatment, disturbed family relationships before illness onset, and marital status (being married) (75, 76). Patients with anorexia nervosa who purge are at much greater risk for developing serious general medical complications (77). In general, adolescents have better outcomes than adults, and younger adolescents have better outcomes than older adolescents (78–80). However, many of these prognostic indicators have not been consistently replicated and may be sturdier predictors of short-term but not long-term outcomes.

2. Bulimia nervosa

Very little is known about the long-term prognosis of patients with untreated bulimia nervosa. Over a 1- to 2-year period, a community sample reported modest degrees of spontaneous improvement, with roughly 25%–30% reductions in binge eating, purging, and laxative abuse (81, 82). The overall short-term success rate for patients receiving psychosocial treatment or medication has been reported to be 50%–70% (70). Relapse rates between 30% and 50% have been reported for successfully treated patients after 6 months to 6 years of follow-up, and some data suggest that slow improvement continues as the period of follow-up extends to 10–15 years (83–86). In a large study of the long-term course of bulimia nervosa patients 6 years after successful treatment in an intensive program (87), outcomes of 60% of the patients were rated as good, 29% were of intermediate success, and 10% were poor, with 1% deceased.

Patients who function well and have milder symptoms at the start of treatment, and who are therefore more likely to be treated as outpatients, often have a better prognosis than those who function poorly and whose disordered eating symptoms are of sufficient severity to merit hospitalization (88). Some studies suggest that higher frequency of pretreatment vomiting is associated with poor outcomes (89, 90). The importance of working on patients' motivation as a preliminary measure before starting other treatments has gained recent attention and has been found to impact the rapidity of response to care (5).

▶ C. EPIDEMIOLOGY

Estimates of the incidence or prevalence of eating disorders vary depending on the sampling and assessment methods. The reported lifetime prevalence of anorexia nervosa among women has ranged from 0.5% for narrowly defined to 3.7% for more broadly defined anorexia nervosa (91, 92). With regard to bulimia nervosa, estimates of the lifetime prevalence among women have ranged from 1.1% to 4.2% (93, 94). Some studies suggest that the prevalence of bulimia nervosa in the United States may have decreased slightly in recent years (95). Eating disorders are more commonly seen among female subjects, with estimates of the male-female prevalence ratio ranging from 1:6 to 1:10 (although 19%–30% of the younger patient populations with anorexia nervosa are male) (96–98). The prevalence of anorexia nervosa and bulimia nervosa in children and younger adolescents is unknown.

In many other countries, there appears to be an overall increase in eating disorders, even in cultures in which the disorder is rare (99). Japan appears to be the only non-Western country that has had a substantial and continuing increase in eating disorders, with figures that are comparable to or above those found in the United States (100, 101). In addition, eating disorder concerns and symptoms appear to be increasing among Chinese women exposed to culture clashes and modernization in cities such as Hong Kong (102, 103). The prevalence of eating disorders appears to be increasing rapidly in other non-English-speaking countries such as Spain, Argentina, and Fiji (104–107).

In the United States, eating disorders appear to be about as common in young Hispanic women as in Caucasians, more common among Native Americans, and less common among blacks and Asians (108). However, several studies in the Southeastern United States (109, 110) have shown that many eating disorder behaviors are even more common among African American women than others. Black women are more likely to develop bulimia nervosa than anorexia nervosa and are more likely to purge with laxatives than by vomiting (111).

It has recently been suggested that in some patients, excessive exercise may precipitate the eating disorder (112, 113). Female athletes in certain sports such as distance running and gymnastics are especially vulnerable. Male bodybuilders are also at risk although the symptom picture often differs, since the bodybuilder may emphasize a wish to "get bigger" and may also abuse anabolic steroids.

First-degree female relatives of patients with anorexia nervosa have higher rates of anorexia nervosa (114) and bulimia nervosa (92, 115). Identical twin siblings of patients with anorexia nervosa or bulimia nervosa also have higher rates of these disorders, with monozygotic twins having higher concordance than dizygotic twins. The evidence regarding rates of bulimia nervosa in other first-degree female relatives remains unclear; some studies report a higher rate among first-degree female relatives while others do not (94). Families of patients with bulimia nervosa have been found to have higher rates of substance abuse (particularly alcoholism) (116, 117), but transmission of substance abuse in these families may be independent of transmission of bulimia nervosa (6). In addition, families of patients with bulimia nervosa have higher rates of affective disorders (116, 118) and obesity (119).

In the psychodynamic literature, patients with anorexia nervosa have been described as having difficulties with separation and autonomy (often manifested as enmeshed relationships with parents), affect regulation (including the direct expression of anger and aggression), and negotiating psychosexual development. These deficits may make women who are predisposed to anorexia nervosa more vulnerable to cultural pressures for achieving a stereotypic body image (17–19, 120, 121).

Patients with bulimia nervosa have been described as having difficulties with impulse regulation resulting from a dearth of parental (usually maternal) involvement. Bulimia nervosa has also been described as a dissociated self-state, as resulting from deficits in self-regulation, and as representing resentful, angry attacks on one's own body out of masochistic/sadistic needs (40, 41).

High rates of comorbid psychiatric illness are found in patients seeking treatment at tertiary psychiatric treatment centers. Comorbid major depression or dysthymia has been reported in 50%–75% of patients with anorexia nervosa (71) and bulimia nervosa (71, 122, 123). Estimates of the prevalence of bipolar disorder among patients with anorexia nervosa or bulimia nervosa are usually around 4%–6% but have been reported to be as high as 13% (124). The lifetime prevalence of obsessive-compulsive disorder (OCD) among anorexia nervosa cases has been as high as 25% (71, 125, 126), and obsessive-compulsive symptoms have been found in a large majority of weight-restored patients with anorexia nervosa treated in tertiary care centers (47). OCD is also common among patients with bulimia nervosa (122). Comorbid anxiety disorders, particularly social phobia, are common among patients with anorexia nervosa and patients with bulimia nervosa (71, 122, 123). Substance abuse has been found in as many as 30%–37% of patients with bulimia nervosa; among patients with anorexia nervosa, estimates of those with substance abuse have ranged from 12% to 18%, with this problem occurring primarily among those with the binge/purge subtype (71, 123).

Comorbid personality disorders are frequently found among patients with eating disorders, with estimates ranging from 42% to 75%. Associations between bulimia nervosa and cluster B and C disorders (particularly borderline personality disorder and avoidant personality disorder) and between anorexia nervosa and cluster C disorders (particularly avoidant personality disorder and obsessive-compulsive personality disorder) have been reported (127). Eating disorder patients with personality disorders are more likely than those without personality disorders to also have concurrent mood or substance abuse disorders (122). Comorbid personality disorders are significantly more common among patients with the binge/purge subtype of anorexia nervosa than the restricting subtype or normal weight patients with bulimia nervosa (128).

Sexual abuse has been reported in 20%–50% of patients with bulimia nervosa (129) and those with anorexia nervosa (130, 131), although sexual abuse may be more common in patients with bulimia nervosa than in those with the restricting subtype of anorexia nervosa (132–134). Childhood sexual abuse histories are reported more often in women with eating disorders than in women from the general population. Women who have eating disorders in the context of sexual abuse appear to have higher rates of comorbid psychiatric conditions than other women with eating disorders (134, 135).

IV. TREATMENT PRINCIPLES AND ALTERNATIVES

In the following sections, the available data on the efficacy of treatments for eating disorders are reviewed. Most studies have consisted of 6–12-week trials designed to evaluate the short-term efficacy of treatments. Unfortunately, there is a scarce amount of data on the long-term effects of treatment for patients with eating disorders, who often have a chronic course and variable long-term prognosis. Many studies also inadequately characterize the phase of illness when patients were first treated, e.g., early or late, which may have an impact on outcomes. In addition, most studies have examined the efficacy of treatments only on eating disorder symptoms; few have examined the effectiveness of treatments on associated features and comorbid conditions such as the persistent mood, anxiety, and personality disorders that are common among "real world" populations.

A variety of outcome measures are employed in trials for patients with eating disorders. Outcome measures in studies of patients with anorexia nervosa primarily are the amount of weight gained within specified time intervals or the proportion of patients achieving a specified percentage of ideal body weight, as well as the return of menses in those with secondary amenorrhea. Measures of the severity or frequency of eating disorder behaviors have also been reported. In studies of bulimia nervosa, outcome measures include reductions in the frequency or severity of eating disorder behaviors and the proportion of patients achieving elimination of or a specific reduction in eating disorder behaviors.

When interpreting the results of studies, particularly for psychosocial interventions that may consist of multiple elements, it may be difficult to identify the element(s) responsible for treatment effects. It is also important to keep in mind when comparing the effects of psychosocial treatments between studies that there may be important variations in the nature of the treatments delivered to patients.

A. TREATMENT OF ANOREXIA NERVOSA

Anorexia nervosa is a complex, serious, and often chronic condition that may require a variety of treatment modalities at different stages of illness and recovery. Specific treatments include nutritional rehabilitation, psychosocial interventions, and medications; all may be used to correct malnutrition, culturally mediated distortions, and psychological, behavioral, and social deficits.

1. Nutritional rehabilitation

a. Goals

The goals of nutritional rehabilitation for seriously underweight patients are to restore weight, normalize eating patterns, achieve normal perceptions of hunger and satiety, and correct biological and psychological sequelae of malnutrition (136). In general, a healthy goal weight is the weight at which normal menstruation and ovulation are restored. For women who had healthy menses and ovulation in the past, one can estimate that healthy weight will be restored at approximately the same weight at which full physical and psychological vigor were present. Assuming that the patient was not obese to start with, restored healthy weight is unlikely to ever be much lower than that. Since some patients continue to menstruate even at low weight (91), and some others never regain menses, a minimum goal weight is often estimated as 90% of ideal weight for height according to standard tables. At that weight, 86% of patients resume menstruating (although not necessarily ovulating) within 6 months (137). Some studies have relied on pelvic sonography to demonstrate the return of a dominant follicle, which indicates that ovulation has returned (138). Others use anthropomorphic measures to estimate the percentage of body fat (approximately 20%–25%) usually needed for normal fertility (139). In premenarchal girls, a healthy goal weight is the weight at which normal physical and sexual development resumes. It is important to use pediatric growth charts to estimate what height and weight the patient might be expected to achieve.

b. Efficacy

Measures of nutritional status include several different standards of ideal body weight, which can be quite variable (140, 141). Some studies calculate the body mass index, a measure that has become standard in studies of obesity and increasingly in eating disorders research as well. This index is calculated with the formula (weight [in kg]/height [in meters]^2). Individuals with body mass indexes <18.5 are considered to be underweight, and body mass indexes ≤17.5, in the presence of the other diagnostic criteria, indicate anorexia nervosa. Body mass indexes are increasingly used in research studies, particularly to compare groups according to percentiles of the body mass index, which take into account height, sex, and age in their calculations (142). However, most clinicians still use standard tables to determine healthy body weights in relation to heights. In children and adolescents, growth curves should be followed and are most useful when longitudinal data are available, since extrapolations from cross-sectional data at one point in time can be misleading. Therefore, for most clinical work, it is reasonable to simply weigh the patient and gauge how far she is from her individually estimated healthy body weight (143).

The efficacy with which weight restoration can be achieved varies with treatment setting. For most severely underweight patients, e.g., patients whose weight is 25%–30% below healthy body weight at the start of treatment, little weight gain will be achieved with outpatient treatment. However, most inpatient weight restoration programs can achieve a weight gain of 2–3 lb/week without compromising the patient's safety. Weight at discharge in relation to the healthy target weight may vary depending on the patient's ability to feed herself, the patient's motivation and ability to participate in aftercare programs, and the adequacy of aftercare, including partial hospitalization. The closer the patient is to ideal body weight before discharge, the less the risk of relapse.

Most outpatient programs find weight gain goals of 0.5–1 lb/week to be realistic, although gains of up to 2 lb/week have been reported in a partial hospital program in which patients are scheduled for 12 hours a day, 7 days a week (144). The latter is solely a step-down program, in which patients had been treated previously as inpatients. The clinicians running the program do not believe that it would work as effectively as a "step-up" program for never-hospitalized patients.

Considerable evidence suggests that with nutritional rehabilitation, other eating disorder symptoms diminish as weight is restored, although not necessarily to the point of disappearing. Clinical experience suggests that with weight restoration, food choices increase, food hoarding decreases, and obsessions about food decrease in frequency and intensity. However, it is by no means certain that abnormal eating habits will improve simply as a function of weight gain (76). There is general agreement that distorted attitudes about weight and shape are least likely to change and that excessive exercise may be one of the last of the behaviors associated with the eating disorder to abate.

Regular structured diets may also enable some patients with anorexia nervosa with associated binge-eating and purging behaviors to improve. For some patients, however, giving up severe dietary restrictions and restraints appears to increase binge-eating behavior, which is often accompanied by compensatory purging.

As weight is regained, changes in associated mood and anxiety symptoms can be expected. Initially, the apathy and lethargy associated with malnourishment may abate. As patients start to recover and feel their bodies getting larger, especially as they approach frightening magical numbers on the scale, they may experience a resurgence of anxious and depressive symptoms, irritability, and sometimes suicidal thoughts. These mood symptoms, non-food-related obsessional thoughts, and compulsive behaviors, while often not eradicated, usually decrease with sustained weight gain.

c. Side effects and toxicity

Although weight gain results in improvement in most of the physiological complications of semistarvation, including improvement in electrolytes, heart and kidney function, and attention and concentration, many adverse physiological and psychological symptoms may appear during weight restoration. Initial refeeding may be associated with mild transient fluid retention. However, patients who abruptly stop taking laxatives or diuretics may experience marked rebound fluid retention for several weeks, presumably from salt and water retention due to the elevated aldosterone levels associated with chronic dehydration. Refeeding edema and bloating are frequent occurrences. In rare instances, congestive heart failure may also develop (145).

Patients may experience abdominal pain and bloating with meals from the delayed gastric emptying that accompanies malnutrition. Excessively rapid refeeding and nasogastric or parenteral feeding may be particularly dangerous due to the potential of inducing severe fluid retention, cardiac arrhythmias, cardiac failure, delirium, or seizures, especially in those with the lowest weights (146, 147). Hypophosphatemia, which can be life threatening, can emerge during refeeding when reserves are depleted (148). Constipation can occur, which can progress to obstipation and acute bowel obstruction. As weight gain progresses, many patients also develop acne and breast tenderness. Many patients become unhappy and demoralized about resulting changes in body shape. Management strategies for dealing with these side effects include careful refeeding (to result in not more than 2–3 lb/week of weight gain aside from simple rehydration); frequent physical examinations; monitoring of serum electrolytes (including sodium, potassium, chloride, bicarbonate, calcium, phosphorus, and magnesium) in patients developing refeeding edema; and forewarning patients about refeeding edema. When nasogastric feeding is necessary, continuous feeding (i.e., over 24 hours) may be less likely than three to four bolus feedings a day to result in metabolic abnormalities or subjective discomfort and may be better tolerated by patients.

d. Implementation

Healthy target weights and expected rates of controlled weight gain should be established (e.g., 2–3 lb/week on inpatient units). Refeeding programs should be implemented in nurturing emotional contexts. Staff should convey to patients their intentions to take care of them and not let them die even when the illness prevents the patients from taking care of themselves. Staff should clearly communicate that they are not seeking to engage in control battles and are not trying to punish patients with aversive techniques. Some positive and negative reinforcements should be built into the program (e.g., required bed rest, exercise restrictions, or restrictions of off-unit privileges; these restrictions are reduced or terminated as target weights and other goals are achieved). Intake levels should usually start at 30–40 kcal/kg per day (approximately 1000–1600 kcal/day). Intake may have to be increased to as high as 70–100 kcal/kg per day for some patients during the weight gain phase. Intake levels during weight maintenance and as needed in children and adolescents for further growth and maturation should be set at 40–60 kcal/kg per day. Kaye and colleagues (149) found that weight-restored patients with anorexia nervosa often require 200–400 calories more than gender-, age-, weight-, and height-matched control subjects to maintain weight. Some of this difference may be due to higher rates of fidgeting and other non-exercise-related energy expenditure in these patients (150). Some patients who require higher caloric intakes are exercising frequently, vomiting, or discarding food, while others may have truly higher metabolic rates or other forms of energy expenditure, e.g., fidgeting. Dietitians can help patients choose their own meals and provide a structured food plan that ensures nutritional adequacy and makes certain that none of the major food groups are avoided.

Some patients are extremely unable to recognize their illness, accept the need for treatment, or tolerate the guilt that would accompany eating, even when performed to sustain their lives. On these rare occasions staff has to take over the responsibilities for providing life-preserving care. Nasogastric feedings are preferable to intravenous feedings and may be experienced positively by some patients—particularly younger patients—who may feel relieved to know that they are being cared for and who, while they cannot bring themselves to eat, are willing to allow physicians to feed them. Total parenteral feeding is required only very rarely and in life-threatening situations.

Forced nasogastric or parenteral feeding can be accompanied by substantial dangers (e.g., severe fluid retention and cardiac failure from rapid refeeding), so these interventions should not be used routinely. In situations where involuntary forced feeding is considered, careful thought should be given to clinical circumstances, family opinion, and relevant legal and ethical dimensions of the patient's treatment.

General medical monitoring during refeeding should include assessment of vital signs, food and fluid intake, and output, if indicated, as well as observation for edema, rapid weight gain (associated primarily with fluid overload), congestive heart failure, and gastrointestinal symptoms. Minerals and electrolytes should also be closely monitored since hypophosphatemia and clinically significant electrolyte imbalances can be life-threatening. Serum potassium levels should be regularly monitored in patients who are persistent vomiters. Hypokalemia should be treated with oral potassium supplementation and rehydration. Serum phosphorus levels may drop precipitously during refeeding from the utilization of phosphorus during anabolism in the face of total body depletion. In such cases phosphorus supplementation will be necessary (146). Patients suspected of artificially increasing their weight should be weighed in the morning after voiding, wearing only a gown; their fluid intake also should be carefully monitored. Assessment of urine specimens obtained at the time of weigh-in for specific gravity may help ascertain the extent to which the measured weight reflects excessive water intake.

Physical activity should be adapted to the food intake and energy expenditure of the patient, taking into account bone mineral density and cardiac function. For the severely underweight, patient exercise should be restricted and always carefully supervised and monitored. Once a safe weight is achieved, the focus of an exercise program should be on physical fitness as opposed to expending calories. The focus on fitness should be balanced with restoring patients' positive relationships with their bodies—helping them to take back control and get pleasure from physical activities rather than being self-critically, even masochistically, enslaved to them. Staff should help patients deal with their concerns about weight gain and body image changes, since these are particularly difficult adjustments for patients to make.

Research that addresses the optimal length of hospitalization is sparse. Two studies have reported that hospitalized patients who are discharged at lower than their target weight subsequently relapse and are rehospitalized at higher rates than those who achieve their target weight. Often, these low-weight discharges were associated with brief lengths of stay. The closer the patient is to ideal weight at the time of discharge from the hospital, the lower the risk of relapse (151, 152). There is no available evidence to show that brief stays for anorexia nervosa are associated with good long-term outcomes.

2. Psychosocial treatments

a. Goals

The goals of psychosocial treatments are to help patients 1) understand and cooperate with their nutritional and physical rehabilitation, 2) understand and change the behaviors and dysfunctional attitudes related to their eating disorder, 3) improve their interpersonal and social functioning, and 4) address comorbid psychopathology and psychological conflicts that reinforce or maintain eating disorder behaviors. Achieving these goals often requires an initial enhancement of patients' motivation to change along with ongoing efforts to sustain this motivation.

b. Efficacy

Few systematic trials of psychosocial therapies have been completed, and a few others are under way. Most evidence for the efficacy of psychosocial therapies comes from case reports or case series (48). Additional evidence comes from the considerable clinical experience that suggests a well-conducted regimen of psychotherapy plays an important role in both ameliorating the symptoms of anorexia nervosa and preventing relapse.

Structured inpatient and partial hospitalization programs. Most inpatient programs employ one of a variety of behaviorally formulated interventions. These behavioral programs commonly provide a combination of nonpunitive reinforcers (e.g., empathic praise, exercise-related limits and rewards, bed rest and privileges linked to achieving weight goals and desired behaviors). Behavioral programs have been shown to produce good short-term therapeutic effects (153). One meta-analysis that compared behavioral psychotherapy programs to treatment with medications alone found that behavior therapy resulted in more consistent weight gain among patients with anorexia nervosa as well as shorter hospital stays (153). Some studies (154, 155) have shown that "lenient" behavioral programs, which utilize initial bed rest and the threat of returning the patient to bed if weight gain does not continue, may be as effective and perhaps in some situations more efficient than "strict" programs, in which meal-by-meal caloric intake or daily weight is tied precisely to a schedule of privileges (e.g., time out of bed, time off the unit, permission to exercise or receive visitors). The use of various modalities considered coercive by patients with anorexia nervosa, for whom control is of such importance, is an issue to be carefully considered. The setting of limits is developmentally appropriate in the management of adolescents and may help shape the patient's behavior in a healthy direction. It is essential for caregivers to be clear about their own intentions and empathic regarding the patients' impressions of being coerced. Caregivers should be seen as using techniques that are not meant as coercive measures but rather are components of a general medical treatment required for the patient's health and survival.

Individual psychotherapy. During the acute phase of treatment, the efficacy of specific psychotherapeutic interventions for facilitating weight gain remains uncertain. Clinical consensus suggests that during acute refeeding and while weight gain is occurring, it is virtually always beneficial to provide patients with individual psychotherapeutic management that is psychodynamically sensitive and informed and that provides empathic understanding, explanations, praise for positive efforts, coaching, support, encouragement, and other positive behavioral reinforcement. During the acute phase of treatment, as well as later on, seeing patients' families is also helpful. For patients who initially lack motivation, psychotherapeutic encounters that employ techniques based on motivational enhancement may help patients increase their awareness and desire for recovery.

On the other hand, attempts to conduct formal psychotherapy with starving patients—who are often negativistic, obsessional, or mildly cognitively impaired—may often be ineffective. Clinical consensus suggests that psychotherapy alone is generally not sufficient to treat severely malnourished patients with anorexia nervosa. While the value of establishing and maintaining a psychotherapeutically informed relationship is clearly beneficial, and psychotherapeutic sessions to enhance motivation and to further weight gain are likely to be helpful, the value of formal psychotherapy during the acute refeeding stage is uncertain (156). As yet, no controlled studies have reported whether cognitive behavior psychotherapy or other specific psychotherapeutic interventions are effective for nutritional recovery. Some practitioners have used various modalities of group psychotherapy programs adjunctively in the treatment of anorexia nervosa (157–159). However, practitioners have also found that group psychotherapy programs conducted during the acute phase among malnourished patients with anorexia nervosa may be ineffective and can sometimes have negative therapeutic effects (e.g., patients may compete for who can be thinnest or exchange countertherapeutic techniques on simulating weight gain or hiding food) (160).

However, once malnutrition has been corrected and weight gain has started, considerable agreement exists that psychotherapy can be very helpful for patients with anorexia nervosa. Although there has been little formal study of its effectiveness, psychotherapy is generally thought to be helpful for patients to understand 1) what they have been through; 2) developmental, family, and cultural antecedents of their illness; 3) how their illness may have been a maladaptive attempt to cope and emotionally self-regulate; 4) how to avoid or minimize risks of relapse; and 5) how to better deal with salient developmental and other important life issues in the future. At present there is no absolute weight or percentage of body fat that indicates when a patient is actually ready to begin formal psychotherapy. However, clinical experience shows that patients often display improved mood, enhanced cognitive functioning, and clear thought processes even before there is substantial weight gain. Many clinicians favor cognitive behavior psychotherapy for maintaining healthy eating behaviors and cognitive or interpersonal psychotherapy for inducing cognitive restructuring and promoting more effective coping (161, 162). Many clinicians also employ psychodynamically oriented individual or group psychotherapy after acute weight restoration to address underlying personality disorders that may contribute to the illness and to foster psychological insight and maturation (18, 19, 42, 121, 163). Thus, verbal or experiential psychotherapeutic interventions can begin as soon as the patient is no longer in a medically compromised state.

In a minority of patients whose refractory anorexia nervosa continues despite notable trials of nutritional rehabilitation, medications, and hospitalizations, more extensive psychotherapeutic measures may be undertaken in further efforts to engage and help motivate them, or, failing that, as compassionate care. This "difficult to treat" subgroup may represent an as yet poorly understood group of patients with malignant, chronic anorexia nervosa. Efforts made to understand and to engage the unique plight of such a patient may sometimes result in engagement in the therapeutic alliance such that the nutritional protocol may begin (18, 19, 120, 164). For patients who have difficulty talking about their problems, clinicians have also tried a variety of nonverbal therapeutic methods, such as creative arts and movement therapy programs, and have reported them to be useful (165). At various stages of recovery, occupational therapy programs may also enhance deficits in self-concept and self-efficacy (166, 167).

Family psychotherapy. Family therapy and couples psychotherapy are frequently useful for both symptom reduction and dealing with family relational problems that may contribute to maintaining the disorder. In one controlled study of patients with anorexia nervosa with onset at or before age 18 and a duration of fewer than 3 years, those treated with family therapy showed greater improvement 1 year after discharge from the hospital than those treated with individual psychotherapy. The 5-year follow-up study showed, quite remarkably, a continuing effect of family therapy (168, 169). The study also points out that family therapy may have more impact for adolescents with eating disorders than for adults. One limitation of this study was that patients were not assigned to receive both family and individual treatment, a combination frequently used in practice.

Particular help should be offered to patients with eating disorders who are themselves mothers. Attention should be paid to their mothering skills and to their offspring to minimize the risk of transmission of eating disorders (170–172).

Psychosocial interventions based on addiction models. Psychosocial interventions based on addiction models. Some clinicians consider that eating disorders may be usefully treated through addiction models, but no data from short- or long-term outcome studies that used these methods have been reported. Some concerns about addiction-oriented programs for eating disorders result from zealous and narrow application of the 12-step philosophy. Clinicians have reported encountering patients who, while attempting to resolve anorexia nervosa by means of 12-step programs alone, could have been greatly helped by adding conventional treatment approaches to the 12-step model, such as medications, nutritional counseling, and psychodynamic or cognitive behavior approaches. By limiting their attempts to recover to 12 steps alone, such patients not only deprive themselves of the potential benefits of conventional treatments but also may expose themselves to misinformation about nutrition and eating disorders offered by well-intentioned nonprofessionals encountered in these groups.

It is important for programs that employ these models to be equipped to care for patients with the substantial psychiatric and general medical problems that are often associated with eating disorders. Some programs attempt to blend features of addiction models, such as the 12 steps, with medical model programs that employ cognitive behavior approaches (173). However, no systematic data exist regarding the effectiveness of these approaches for any patients with anorexia nervosa.

Support groups.   Support groups led by professionals or by advocacy organizations are available and provide patients and their families with mutual support, advice, and education about eating disorders. These groups may be of adjunctive benefit in combination with other treatment modalities. Patients and their families are increasingly using on-line web sites, news groups, and chat rooms as resources. While a substantial amount of worthwhile information and support are available in this fashion, lack of professional supervision may sometimes lead to misinformation and unhealthy dynamics among users. Clinicians should inquire about the use of electronic support and other alternative and complementary approaches and be prepared to discuss information and ideas that patients and their families have gathered from these sources.

c.   Implementation

Although a variety of different management models are used for patients with anorexia nervosa, there are no data available on their efficacies. When competent to do so, the psychiatrist should manage both the general medical and psychiatric needs of the patient. Some programs routinely arrange for interdisciplinary team management (sometimes called split management) models of treatment, wherein a psychiatrist writes orders, handles administrative and general medical requirements, and prescribes behavioral techniques intended to change the disturbed eating and weight patterns. Other clinicians then provide the psychotherapeutic intervention (in the form of cognitive behavior psychotherapy, psychodynamic psychotherapy, or family therapy) with the patient alone or in a group. For this management model to work effectively, all personnel must work closely together, maintaining open communication and mutual respect to avoid reinforcing some patients' tendencies to play staff off each other, i.e., to split the staff.

An alternative interdisciplinary management approach has general medical care providers (e.g., specialists in internal medicine, pediatrics, adolescent medicine, and nutrition) manage general medical issues, such as nutrition, weight gain, exercise, and eating patterns, while the psychiatrist addresses the psychiatric issues. In adolescence, the biopsychosocial nature of anorexia nervosa and bulimia nervosa especially indicates the need for interdisciplinary treatment. Each aspect of care must be developmentally tailored to the treatment of adolescents (174).

3. Medications

a.   Goals

Medications are used most frequently after weight has been restored to maintain weight and normal eating behaviors as well as treat psychiatric symptoms associated with anorexia nervosa.

b.   Efficacy

Antidepressants.   Studies of antidepressants for restoration of weight are limited, and these medications are not routinely used in the acute phase of treatment for severely malnourished patients. One recent controlled study (175) showed no advantage for adding fluoxetine to nutritional and psychosocial interventions in the treatment of hospitalized, malnourished patients with anorexia nervosa with respect to either the amount or the speed of weight recovery. Results from an uncontrolled trial (176) suggest that fluoxetine may help some treatment-resistant patients with weight restoration, but many patients will not be helped.

Antidepressants may be considered after weight gain when the psychological effects of malnutrition are resolving, since these medications have been shown to be helpful with weight maintenance (149). In one controlled trial, weight-restored patients with anorexia nervosa who took fluoxetine (average 40 mg/day) after hospital discharge had less weight loss, depression, and fewer rehospitalizations for anorexia nervosa during the subsequent year than those who received placebo. Few other controlled studies of antidepressant treatment of anorexia nervosa have been published. In an open outpatient study (177), those treated with psychotherapy plus citalopram did worse (losing several kilograms) than underweight anorexia nervosa patients treated with psychotherapy alone (whose weights dropped about 0.2 kg during the period of observation), which suggests that this SSRI medication was counterproductive for this population. In one study (178), lower-weight patients with the restricting subtype of anorexia who were receiving intensive inpatient treatment seemed to benefit, albeit to a small degree, from a combination of amitriptyline and cyproheptadine. In another study (179), no significant beneficial effect was observed from adding clomipramine to the usual treatment (although doses of only 50 mg/day were used).

SSRIs are commonly considered for patients with anorexia nervosa whose depressive, obsessive, or compulsive symptoms persist in spite of or in the absence of weight gain.

Other medications.   Few controlled studies have been published on the use of other psychotropic medications for the treatment of anorexia nervosa. In one study (180), lithium carbonate resulted in no substantial benefit. Another study suggested no significant benefit for pimozide (181).

Other psychotropic medications are most often used to treat psychiatric symptoms that may be associated with anorexia nervosa. Examples include low doses of neuroleptics for marked obsessionality, anxiety, and psychotic-like thinking and antianxiety agents used selectively before meals to reduce anticipatory anxiety concerning eating (58, 182). Although there are no controlled studies to support effectiveness, eating disorders clinicians are increasingly using low doses of newer novel antipsychotic medications together with SSRIs or other new antidepressants in treating highly obsessional and compulsive patients with anorexia nervosa.

Other somatic treatments, ranging from vitamin and hormone treatments to electroconvulsive therapy, have been tried in uncontrolled studies. None has been shown to have specific value in the treatment of anorexia nervosa symptoms (183). Although estrogen replacement is sometimes used in anorexia nervosa patients with chronic amenorrhea to reduce calcium loss and thereby reduce the risks of osteoporosis (52), existing evidence in support of hormone replacement therapy for the treatment or prevention of osteopenia in women with anorexia nervosa is marginal at best. Estrogen replacement has not been evaluated in children or adolescents. Seeman and colleagues (184) reported that the lumbar bone mineral density of women with anorexia nervosa who were taking oral contraceptives was significantly higher than that of patients not supplemented with estrogen, although the bone mineral density in both groups remained below normal for age. In preliminary studies (185, 186), hormone replacement therapy did not effectively improve bone mass density. The only controlled trial to date that looked at the effects of estrogen administration on women with anorexia nervosa showed that estrogen-treated patients had no significant change in bone mass density compared to control subjects. However, a subgroup of the estrogen-treated patients whose initial body weight was less than 70% of their ideal weight had a 4.0% increase in mean bone density, whereas subjects of comparable body weight not treated with estrogen had a further 20.1% decrease in bone density. This finding suggests that hormone replacement therapy may help a subset of low-weight women with anorexia nervosa (54). At the same time, artificially inducing menses carries the risk of supporting or reinforcing a patient's denial that she does not need to gain weight. On the other hand, weight rehabilitation has been shown to be an effective means of increasing bone mineral density (51, 187). To summarize, estrogen alone does not generally appear to reverse osteoporosis or osteopenia, and unless there is weight gain, it does not prevent further bone loss. Before offering estrogen, many clinicians stress that efforts should first be made to increase weight and achieve resumption of normal menses (188).

Furthermore, at the present time there is no evidence that any of the new treatments for postmenopausal osteoporosis, such as biphosphonates, are effective for treating osteoporosis in patients with anorexia nervosa (189). However, studies concerning these medications, bone growth factors, and other investigative treatments are now under way. If fracture risk is substantial, patients should be cautioned to avoid high-impact exercises.

Pro-motility agents such as metoclopramide are commonly offered for the bloating and abdominal pains due to gastroparesis and premature satiety seen in the some patients.

c. Side effects and toxicity

Many clinicians report that malnourished depressed patients are more prone to side effects and less responsive to the beneficial effects of tricyclics, SSRIs, and other novel antidepressant medications than depressed patients of normal weight. For example, the use of tricyclics may be associated with greater risks of hypotension, increased cardiac conduction times, and arrhythmia, particularly in purging patients whose hydration may be inadequate and whose cardiac status may be nutritionally compromised. Although fluoxetine has been found to impair appetite and cause weight loss in normal weight and obese patients at higher doses, this effect has not been reported in anorexia nervosa patients treated with lower doses. Citalopram has been associated with additional weight loss in anorexia nervosa (177). Because of the reported higher seizure risk associated with bupropion in purging patients, this medication should not be used in such patients (190, 191).

Strategies to manage side effects include limiting the use of medications to patients with persistent depression, anxiety, or obsessive-compulsive symptoms; using low initial doses in underweight patients; and being very vigilant about side effects. Given other alternatives, tricyclic antidepressants should be avoided in underweight patients and in patients who are at risk for suicide. In patients for whom there is a concern regarding potential cardiovascular effects of medication, cardiovascular consultations to evaluate status and to advise on the use of medication may be helpful.

d. Implementation

Because anorexia nervosa symptoms and associated features such as depression may remit with weight gain, decisions concerning the use of medications should often be deferred until weight has been restored. Antidepressants can be considered for weight maintenance. The decision to use medications and which medications to choose will be determined by the remaining symptom picture (e.g., antidepressants are usually considered for those with persistent depression, anxiety, or obsessive-compulsive symptoms).

▶ B. TREATMENT OF BULIMIA NERVOSA

Strategies for the treatment of bulimia nervosa include nutritional counseling and rehabilitation; psychosocial interventions (including cognitive behavior, interpersonal, behavioral, psychodynamic, and psychoanalytic approaches) in individual or group format; family interventions; and medications.

1. Nutritional rehabilitation

Reducing binge eating and purging are primary goals in treating bulimia nervosa. Because most patients described in the bulimia nervosa psychotherapy treatment literature have been of normal weight, weight restoration is usually not a focus of therapy as it is with patients with anorexia nervosa. Even if they are within statistically normal ranges, many patients with bulimia nervosa weigh less than their appropriate biologically determined set points (or set ranges) and may have to gain some weight to achieve physiological and emotional stability. These patients require the establishment of a pattern of regular, non-binge meals, with attention paid to increasing their caloric intake and expanding macronutrient selection. Although many patients with bulimia nervosa report irregular menses, improvement in menstrual function has not been systematically assessed in the available outcome studies.

Even among patients of normal weight, nutritional counseling can be used to accomplish a variety of goals, such as reducing behaviors related to the eating disorder, minimizing food restriction, correcting nutritional deficiencies, increasing the variety of foods eaten, and encouraging healthy but not excessive exercise patterns. There is some evidence that treatment programs that include dietary counseling and management as part of the program are more effective than those that do not (192).

2. Psychosocial treatments

a. Goals

The goals of psychosocial interventions vary and can include the following: reduction in, or elimination of, binge-eating and purging behaviors; improvement in attitudes related to the eating disorder; minimization of food restriction; increasing the variety of foods eaten; encouragement of healthy but not excessive exercise patterns; treatment of comorbid conditions and clinical features associated with eating disorders; and addressing themes that may underlie eating disorder behaviors such as developmental issues, identity formation, body image concerns, self-esteem in areas outside of those related to weight and shape, sexual and aggressive difficulties, affect regulation, gender role expectations, family dysfunction, coping styles, and problem solving.

b. Efficacy

Individual psychotherapy.   Cognitive behavioral psychotherapy, specifically directed at the eating disorder symptoms and underlying cognitions in patients with bulimia nervosa, is the psychosocial intervention that has been most intensively studied and for which there is the most evidence of efficacy (43, 192–209). Significant decrements in binge eating, vomiting, and laxative abuse have been documented among some patients receiving cognitive behavior therapy; however, the percentage of patients who achieve full abstinence from binge/purge behavior is variable and often includes only a minority of patients (43, 193, 195–199, 201, 202, 204, 206). Among studies with control arms, cognitive behavior therapy has been shown to be superior to waiting list (43, 195, 198, 202), minimal intervention (206), or nondirective control (201) conditions. In most of the published cognitive behavior therapy trials, significant improvements in either self-reported (198, 210) or clinician-rated (200) mood have been reported.

In practice, many other types of individual psychotherapy are employed in the treatment of bulimia nervosa, such as interpersonal, psychodynamically oriented, or psychoanalytic approaches. Clinical experience also suggests that these approaches can help in the treatment of the comorbid mood, anxiety, personality, interpersonal, and trauma- or abuse-related disorders that frequently accompany bulimia nervosa (211). Evidence for the efficacy of these treatments for bulimia nervosa comes mainly from case reports and case series. Some modes of therapy, including the interpersonal and psychodynamic approaches, have also been studied in randomized trials as comparison treatments for cognitive behavior therapy or in separate trials (196, 199, 212). In general, these and other studies have shown interpersonal psychotherapy to be helpful. The specific forms of focused psychodynamic psychotherapy that have been studied in direct comparison to cognitive behavior therapy have generally not been as effective as cognitive behavior therapy in short-term trials (213, 214).

Behavioral therapy, which consists of procedures of exposure (e.g., to binge eating food) plus response prevention (e.g., inhibiting vomiting after eating), has also been considered as treatment for bulimia nervosa. However, the evidence regarding the efficacy of this approach is conflicting, as studies have reported enhanced (215), not significantly altered (216), and reduced (193) responses to cognitive behavior therapy when behavioral therapy was used as an adjunct. On the basis of results from a large clinical trial, and given its logistical complexity, exposure treatment does not appear to have additive benefits over a solid core of cognitive behavior therapy (115).

Very few studies have directly compared the effectiveness of various types of individual psychotherapy for treatment of bulimia nervosa. One study by Fairburn and colleagues that compared cognitive behavior therapy, interpersonal psychotherapy, and behavior therapy showed that all three treatments were effective in reducing binge-eating symptoms by the end of treatment, but cognitive behavior therapy was most effective in improving disturbed attitudes toward shape and weight and restrictive dieting (196, 197, 213, 214, 217, 218). However, at long-term follow-up (mean=5.8 years), the study found equal efficacy for interpersonal psychotherapy and cognitive behavior therapy on eating variables, attitudes about shape and weight, and restrictive dieting (218), which suggests that interpersonal psychotherapy patients had "caught up" in terms of benefits over time. An ongoing multicenter study (39) has basically replicated these findings.

Group psychotherapy.   Group psychotherapy approaches have also been used to treat bulimia nervosa. A meta-analysis of 40 group treatment studies suggested moderate efficacy, with those studies that reported 1-year follow-up data reporting that improvement was typically maintained (205). There is some evidence that group treatment programs that include dietary counseling and management as part of the program are more effective than those that do not (192), and that frequent visits early in treatment (e.g., sessions several times a week initially) result in improved outcome (196, 197, 204). Many clinicians favor a combination of individual and group psychotherapy. Psychodynamic and cognitive behavior approaches may be combined. Group therapy may help patients to more effectively deal with the shame surrounding their disease as well as provide additional peer-based feedback and support.

Family and marital therapy.   Family therapy has been reported to be helpful in the treatment of bulimia nervosa in a large case series, but more systematic studies are not available (207). Family therapy should be considered whenever possible, especially for adolescents who still live with their parents, older patients with ongoing conflicted interactions with parents, or patients with marital discord. For women with eating disorders who are mothers, parenting help and interventions aimed at assessing and, if necessary, aiding their children should be included (170–172).

Support groups/12-step programs.   Considerable controversy exists regarding the role of 12-step programs as the sole intervention in the treatment of eating disorders, primarily because these programs do not address nutritional considerations or the complex psychological/behavioral deficits of patients with eating disorders. Twelve-step programs or other approaches that exclusively focus on the need for abstinence without attending to nutritional considerations or behavioral deficits are not recommended as the sole initial treatment approach for bulimia nervosa.

Some patients have found Overeaters Anonymous and similar groups to be helpful as adjuncts to initial treatments or for preventing subsequent relapses (203, 219), but no data from short- or long-term outcome studies of these programs have been reported. Because of the great variability of knowledge, attitudes, beliefs, and practices from chapter to chapter and from sponsor to sponsor regarding eating disorders and their general medical and psychotherapeutic treatment, and because of the great variability of patients' personality structures, clinical conditions, and susceptibility to potential countertherapeutic practices, clinicians should carefully monitor patients' experiences with these programs.

c. Side effects and toxicity

Patients occasionally have difficulty with certain elements of psychotherapy. For example, among patients receiving cognitive behavior therapy, some are quite resistant to self-monitoring while others have difficulty mastering cognitive restructuring. Many patients are initially resistant to changing their eating behaviors, particularly when it comes to increasing their caloric intake or reducing exercise. However, complete lack of acceptance of the approach appears to be rare, although this has not been systematically studied.

Management strategies to deal with potential negative effects of psychotherapeutic interventions include 1) careful pretreatment evaluation, during which time the therapist must assess and enhance the patient's level of motivation for change and identify appropriate candidates for a given approach and format (e.g., individual versus group); 2) being alert to a patient's reactions to and attitudes about the proposed treatment and listening to and discussing the patient's concerns in a supportive fashion; 3) ongoing monitoring of the quality of the therapeutic relationship; and 4) identification of patients for whom another treatment should be coadministered or given before psychotherapy begins (e.g., chemical dependency treatment for those actively abusing alcohol or other drugs, antidepressant treatment for patients whose depression makes them unable to become actively involved, more intensive psychotherapy for those with severe personality disorders, and group therapy for those not previously participating). Alternative strategies may be necessary to move the therapeutic process forward and to prevent abrupt termination of therapy.

d. Implementation

A review of the literature shows that the way in which psychotherapy has been implemented varies, in some cases considerably. For cognitive behavior therapy, several controlled trials used fairly short-term, time-limited interventions, such as 20 individual psychotherapy sessions over 16 weeks, with two scheduled visits per week for the first 4 weeks (193, 196, 197, 213, 214, 217, 218, 220–222). Some investigators have examined whether more than one visit per week is needed, particularly early in treatment. In one study of group cognitive behavior psychotherapy (204), additional visits early in treatment or twice weekly visits throughout treatment were both superior regimens to one psychotherapy session per week.

A growing literature has suggested that cognitive behavior therapy can be administered successfully through self-help or guided self-help manuals, at times in association with pharmacotherapy (223–227). While such techniques are not yet sufficiently developed to recommend their acceptance as a primary treatment strategy, developments in this area may prove of great importance in providing treatment to patients who otherwise might not have access to adequate care. Clinicians unfamiliar with the cognitive behavior therapy approach may benefit from acquainting themselves with these treatment manuals and obtaining specialized training in cognitive behavior therapy to further help their bulimia nervosa patients by using such manuals in treatment (213, 228–233).

This section has presented the results of cognitive behavior therapy and other short-term treatments, since these treatments have been the subject of the preponderance of studies. However, the field is in great need of well-conducted studies that examine other treatment approaches, particularly psychodynamically informed therapies. In addition, most available studies report relatively short-term results. Better studies are needed of the long-term effectiveness of these as well as other psychotherapeutic approaches, particularly for the complex presentations with multiple comorbid conditions that are usually seen in psychiatric practice.

3. Medications

a. Goals

Medications, primarily antidepressants, are used to reduce the frequency of disturbed eating behaviors such as binge eating and vomiting. In addition, pharmacotherapy is employed to alleviate symptoms that may accompany disordered eating behaviors, such as depression, anxiety, obsessions, or certain impulse disorder symptoms.

b. Antidepressants

Efficacy. The observation that some patients with bulimia nervosa were clinically depressed led to the first uses of antidepressants in the acute phase of treatment (234). However, later randomized trials demonstrated that non-depressed patients also responded to these medications and that baseline presence of depression was not a predictor of medication response (235–237). Although wide variability exists across studies, reductions in binge eating and vomiting rates in the range of 50%–75% have been achieved with active medication (191, 238–252). The available studies also suggest that antidepressants improve associated comorbid disorders and complaints such as mood and anxiety symptoms. Some studies show improved interpersonal functioning with medication as well. Specific antidepressant agents that have demonstrated efficacy among patients with bulimia nervosa in double-blind, placebo-controlled studies include tricyclic compounds such as imipramine (234, 253), desipramine (235, 254–256), and amitriptyline (for mood but not eating variables) (236); the SSRI fluoxetine (242–244); several MAOIs, including phenelzine (237), isocarboxazide (257), and brofaramine (for vomiting but not binge eating) (258); and several other antidepressants, including mianserin (252), bupropion (191), and trazodone (250). (Bupropion, however, was associated with seizures in purging bulimic patients, so its use is not recommended.) One study (251) suggests that patients with atypical depression and bulimia nervosa may preferentially respond to phenelzine in comparison with imipramine. However, since MAOIs are potentially dangerous in patients with chaotic eating and purging, great caution should be exercised in their use for bulimia nervosa. To date, the only medication approved by the Food and Drug Administration for bulimia nervosa is fluoxetine.

Two trials have examined the utility of antidepressant maintenance therapy. One trial with fluvoxamine (240) demonstrated an attenuated relapse rate versus placebo in patients with bulimia nervosa who were on a maintenance regimen of the medication after leaving an inpatient treatment program; however, in the continuation arm of a clinical trial with desipramine (256), 29% of the patients entering that phase experienced a relapse within 4 months. Trials using fluoxetine for relapse prevention are currently under way.

Side effects and toxicity.   Side effects vary widely across studies depending on the type of antidepressant medication used. For the tricyclic antidepressants, common side effects include sedation, constipation, dry mouth, and, with amitriptyline, weight gain (234–236, 253–255). The toxicity of tricyclic antidepressants in overdose, up to and including death, also dictates caution in patients who are at risk for suicide. In the first multicenter fluoxetine trial (242), the most common side effects at 60 mg/day were insomnia (30%), nausea (28%), and asthenia (23%). In the second multicenter study (244), the most common side effects were insomnia (35%), nausea (30%), and asthenia (21%). Sexual side effects are also common in patients receiving SSRIs. Studies using various other medications have reported substantial dropout rates, although attrition rates across clinical trials have varied dramatically, and the degree to which medication side effects are the cause of high dropout rates has not been defined. Other common contributors to dropping out of clinical trials may involve subtle interpersonal and psychodynamic factors in the physician-patient relationships, which if left unaddressed will also contribute to treatment resistance. The quality of collaboration between patient and clinician is key to success in medication trials (259).

For patients with bulimia nervosa who require mood stabilizers, lithium carbonate is problematic, since lithium levels may shift markedly with rapid volume changes. Both lithium carbonate and valproic acid frequently lead to undesirable weight gains. Selection of a mood stabilizer that avoids these problems may result in better compliance and effectiveness.

No clear risk factors for the development of side effects among patients with bulimia nervosa have been identified. As in most clinical situations, careful preparation of the patient regarding possible side effects and their symptomatic management if they develop should be employed (e.g., stool softeners for constipation).

Implementation.   Often, several different antidepressant medications may have to be tried sequentially to achieve the optimum effect. Doses of tricyclic and MAOI antidepressants for treating patients with bulimia nervosa parallel those used to treat patients with depression, although fluoxetine at doses higher than those used for depression may be more effective for bulimic symptoms (e.g., 60–80 mg/day). The first multicenter fluoxetine study (242) demonstrated that 60 mg was clearly superior to 20 mg on most variables, and in the second study (244) all subjects receiving active medication started with 60 mg. The medication was surprisingly well tolerated at this dose, and many clinicians initiate treatment for bulimia nervosa with fluoxetine at the higher dose, titrating downward if necessary due to side effects.

In cases where symptoms do not respond to medication, it is important to assess whether the patient has taken the medication shortly before vomiting. Serum levels of medication may be obtained to determine whether presumably effective levels have actually been achieved. One study (235) suggested that desipramine serum levels similar to those targeted in depression studies are most therapeutic in patients with bulimia nervosa, but in general serum level/response data have not been presented.

There are few reports on the use of antidepressant medications in the maintenance phase. Available data suggest high rates of relapse while taking medication and possibly higher rates when medications are withdrawn (256). In the absence of more systematic data, most clinicians recommend continuing antidepressant therapy for a minimum of 6 months and probably for a year in most patients with bulimia nervosa.

c. Other medications

A number of other medications have been used experimentally for bulimia nervosa without evidence of efficacy, including fenfluramine (239) and lithium carbonate (245). Fenfluramine has now been taken off the market because of associations between its use (mainly in combination with phentermine) and cardiac valvular abnormalities. Lithium continues to be used occasionally as an adjunct for the treatment of comorbid conditions. The opiate antagonist naltrexone has been studied in three randomized trials at doses used for narcotic addiction and for relapse prevention in alcohol abuse (50–120 mg/day). The results consistently show that the medication is not superior to placebo in the reduction of bulimic symptoms (238, 246, 249). In a small, double-blind crossover study involving higher doses (e.g., 200–300 mg/day), naltrexone did appear to have some efficacy. Further studies using these dose ranges are needed. However, there have been mixed reports concerning the risk of hepatotoxicity with the use of high doses (247, 248, 260).

4. Combinations of psychosocial and medication treatment

Six studies have examined the relative efficacy of psychotherapy, medication, or both in the treatment of bulimia nervosa. In the first study (261), intensive group cognitive psychotherapy (45 hours of therapy over 10 weeks) was superior to imipramine alone in reducing symptoms of binge eating and purging and symptoms of depression. Imipramine plus intensive group cognitive behavior therapy did not improve the outcome on eating variables but did improve depression and anxiety variables. In the second study (262), patients in group cognitive behavior therapy improved more than those receiving desipramine alone. Some advantage was also seen for combination therapy on some variables, such as dietary restraint. The third study (263), which compared fluoxetine treatment, cognitive behavior therapy, and combination therapy, favored cognitive behavior therapy alone and suggested little benefit for combination therapy. Results of this study are difficult to interpret because of a high attrition rate (50% by the 1-month follow-up). In the fourth study (264), cognitive behavior therapy was superior to supportive psychotherapy; active medication (consisting of desipramine, followed by fluoxetine if abstinence from binge eating and purging was not achieved) was superior to placebo in reducing eating disorder behaviors. The combination of cognitive behavior therapy and active medication resulted in the highest abstinence rates. The use of sequential medication in this study addressed a limitation of earlier studies in that typically when one antidepressant fails, a clinician tries other agents, which often result in better antidepressant efficacy than seen with the first medication alone. In the fifth study (241), no advantage was found for the use of fluoxetine over placebo in an inpatient setting, although both groups improved significantly. In the sixth study (265), combination treatment with desipramine and cognitive behavior therapy was terminated prematurely because of a high dropout rate.

In conclusion, the studies suggest that target symptoms such as binge eating and purging and attitudes related to the eating disorder generally respond better to cognitive behavior therapy than pharmacotherapy (261–263), with at least two studies (262, 264) showing that the combination of cognitive behavior therapy and medication is superior to either alone. Two of the studies suggest a greater improvement in mood and anxiety variables when antidepressant therapy is added to cognitive behavior therapy (261, 264). Of note, many experienced clinicians do not find cognitive behavior therapy to be as useful as described by researchers. This may be due to several factors, including clinician inexperience or discomfort with the methods or differences between patients seen in the community and those who have participated as research subjects in these studies.

V. CLINICAL AND ENVIRONMENTAL FEATURES INFLUENCING TREATMENT

▶ ## A. OTHER IMPORTANT CLINICAL FEATURES OF EATING DISORDERS

1. Eating disorder not otherwise specified

Eating disorder not otherwise specified is a commonly used diagnosis, given to nearly 50% of patients with eating disorders who present to tertiary care eating disorders programs. Eating disorder not otherwise specified appears to be particularly common among adolescents. This heterogeneous group of patients largely consists of subsyndromal cases of anorexia nervosa or bulimia nervosa (e.g., those who fail to meet one criterion, such as not having 3 months of amenorrhea or having fewer binge eating episodes per week than required for strictly defined diagnosis). One variant of eating disorder not otherwise specified consists of abusers of weight reduction medications who are trying to lose excessive amounts of weight for cosmetic reasons. In general, the nature and intensity of treatment depends on the symptom profile and severity of impairment, not the DSM-IV diagnosis.

One diagnosis within the eating disorder not otherwise specified category is binge-eating disorder. Although it is not an approved DSM-IV diagnosis at this time, there are research criteria listed in DSM-IV, which consist of disturbances in one or more of the following spheres: behavioral (e.g., binge eating), somatic (e.g., obesity is common although not required), and psychological (e.g., body image dissatisfaction, low self-esteem, depression) (8). Although binge-eating disorder appears to be relatively rare in community cohorts (2% prevalence), it is common among patients seeking treatment for obesity at hospital-affiliated weight programs (30% prevalence) (266). About one-third of these patients are male. Binge-eating disorder occurs much more frequently in adults than in adolescents. Strategies for the treatment of binge-eating disorder include nutritional counseling and dietary management; individual or group behavioral, cognitive behavior, interpersonal, or psychodynamic psychotherapy; and medications.

a. Nutritional rehabilitation and counseling; effect of diet programs on weight

Very-low-calorie diets in patients with binge-eating disorder have been associated with substantial initial weight losses, with over one-third of these patients maintaining their weight loss 1 year after treatment (267–270). Very-low-calorie diets employed together with group behavioral weight control have been effective in reducing binge eating during the period of fasting but may be less effective during or following refeeding (267, 268, 270). However, since such dieting may disinhibit eating and lead to compensatory overeating and binge eating (271), and since chronic calorie restriction can also increase symptoms of depression, anxiety, and irritability (46), new alternative therapies that use a nondiet approach by focusing on self-acceptance, improving body image, better nutrition and health, and increased physical movement and not on weight loss have been developed (272–274). Studies that compared traditional behavioral weight loss programs with nondieting programs have found similar rates of maintained weight loss, with the nondiet programs also producing significant reductions in symptoms related to binge eating, depression, anxiety, bulimia, drive for thinness, and body dissatisfaction (275, 276). Patients with histories of repeated weight loss attempts followed by weight gain (so-called "yo-yo" dieting) or patients with an early onset of binge eating might benefit from following programs that focus on decreasing binge eating rather than weight loss (277, 278).

b. Psychosocial treatments

Cognitive behavior therapy, behavior therapy, and interpersonal therapy have all been associated with binge frequency reduction rates of two-thirds or more and significant abstinence rates during active treatment. However, deterioration during the follow-up period has been observed with all three forms of psychotherapy. Behavior therapy, but not cognitive behavior therapy, has generally been associated with a significant initial weight loss that is then partially regained during the first year following treatment (279–287). This pattern of weight regain after initial weight loss is common in all general medical and psychological treatments for obesity, not only for obesity associated with binge-eating disorder. One 6-year study (288) that followed intensively treated patients with binge-eating disorder found that approximately 57% had good outcomes, 35% intermediate outcomes, and 6% had poor outcomes; 1% had died. Self-help programs using self-guided professionally designed manuals have been effective in reducing the symptoms of binge-eating disorder in the short run for some patients and may sometimes have long-term benefit (289). Addiction-based 12-step approaches, self-help organizations, or treatment programs based on the Alcoholics Anonymous model have been tried, but no systematic outcome studies of these programs are available.

c. Medications

It must be pointed out that medication treatment studies of binge-eating disorder have generally reported very high placebo response rates (around 70%) (238, 290). These high placebo response rates suggest that great caution is needed in evaluating claims of effective treatments, particularly in studies that use only a waiting list control condition.

Medications, primarily antidepressants, have been used in the treatment of binge-eating disorder and related syndromes. Tricyclic antidepressants and fluvoxamine have been associated with reductions of 63%–90% in binge frequency during 2–3 months of treatment (238, 291–293). Naltrexone has been associated with a decrease in binge frequency on the same order (73%), although this rate did not differ from the response to placebo (238). Patients tend to relapse after medication is discontinued (290, 293).

Although the appetite suppressant medications fenfluramine and dexfenfluramine have also been found to significantly reduce binge frequency (290), their use has been associated with serious adverse events, including a

23-fold increase in the risk of developing primary pulmonary hypertension when used for longer than 3 months (294). Very recent studies suggest that patients taking the combination of fenfluramine and phentermine may be at greater risk of heart valve deformation and pulmonary hypertension; as a result, fenfluramine has been withdrawn from the market (294–297). Studies in animals indicate that fenfluramine and dexfenfluramine may be associated with persistent serotonergic neurotoxicity (298, 299).

d. Combined psychosocial and medication treatment strategies

In most studies, the co-administration of medication with psychotherapy has been found to be associated with significantly more weight loss than with psychotherapy alone (280, 300).

2. Chronicity of eating disorders

Many patients who have a chronic course of anorexia nervosa, extending for a decade or more, are unable to maintain a healthy weight and suffer from chronic depression, obsessionality, and social withdrawal. Individualized treatment planning and careful case management are necessary for such chronic patients. Treatment may require consultation with other specialists, repeated hospitalizations, partial hospitalizations, residential care, individual or group therapy, other social therapies, trials of various medications as indicated, and, occasionally, ECT in patients who are seriously depressed. Communication among professionals is especially important throughout the outpatient care of such patients. With chronic patients, small progressive gains and fewer relapses may be the goals of psychological interventions. More frequent outpatient contact and other supports may sometimes help prevent further hospitalizations. Expectations for weight gain with hospitalization may be more modest for chronic patients. Achieving a safe weight compatible with life rather than a healthy weight may be all that is possible. Focusing on quality-of-life issues, rather than change in weight or normalization of eating, and providing compassionate care may be all one can realistically achieve (21, 301).

▶ B. OTHER PSYCHIATRIC FACTORS

1. Substance abuse/dependence

Substance abuse/dependence is common among women with eating disorders (6). Among individuals with bulimia nervosa, 22.9% have been observed to meet criteria for alcohol abuse (302). Substance abuse appears to be less common among restricting patients with anorexia nervosa than among those having the binge-eating/purge type (123, 303, 304). For example, one recent prospective, longitudinal study (305) found bulimic anorectic women to be seven times more likely to develop substance abuse problems than restricting anorectic patients. Patients with comorbid substance abuse and eating disorders appear to have more severe problems with impulsivity in general, including greater risks of shoplifting, suicide gestures, and laxative abuse (135, 304, 306). Available studies indicate that eating disorder patients with a history of prior but currently inactive substance abuse respond to standard therapies in the same manner as those without such a history (307–309) and do not appear to experience exacerbations of their substance abuse disorders after successful treatment (308). However, the presence of a currently active co-morbid substance abuse problem does have implications for treatment. A study of 70 patients with comorbid eating disorders and substance abuse found that the associated axis III medical disorders reflected complications of both eating disorders and substance abuse disorders. Patients with comorbid eating and substance abuse disorders required longer inpatient stays and were less compliant with treatment following hospitalization than those with sub-stance abuse disorders alone (310). Where treatment staff are competent to treat both disorders, concurrent treatment should be attempted.

2. Mood and anxiety disorders

A very high percentage of treatment-seeking patients with eating disorders report a lifetime history of unipolar depression (124, 311, 312). Nutritional insufficiency and weight loss often predispose patients to symptoms of de-pression (46). Depressed individuals with an eating disorder experience great-er levels of anxiety, guilt, and obsessionality, but less social withdrawal and lack of interest, than depressed individuals without eating disorders (313). Several studies suggest that the presence of comorbid depression at initial presentation has minimal or no predictive value for treatment outcome (84). However, the experience of many clinicians suggests that severe depression can impair a patient's ability to become meaningfully involved in psychother-apy and may dictate the need for medication treatment for the mood symptoms from the beginning of treatment.

Lifetime prevalence rates for anxiety disorders also appear to be higher for patients with both anorexia nervosa and bulimia nervosa, but rates for specific anxiety disorders vary (122). In patients with anorexia nervosa, social phobia and OCD are the anxiety disorders most commonly described. For those with bulimia nervosa, comorbid presentations of social phobia, OCD, or simple phobia are most often described. Overanxious disorders of childhood are also common in both anorexia nervosa and bulimia nervosa and precede the onset of these eating disorders (314). Although there is no clear evidence that comorbid anxiety disorders impact significantly on eating disorder treatment outcome, such comorbid problems should be addressed in treatment planning.

3. Personality disorders

The reported prevalence of personality disorders has varied widely across eating disorders and across studies. Individuals with anorexia nervosa tend to have higher rates of cluster C personality disorders, while normal weight patients with bulimia nervosa are more likely to display features of cluster B disorders, particularly impulsive, affective, and narcissistic trait disturbances (128, 315–320). The presence of borderline personality disorder seems to be associated with a greater disturbance in eating attitudes, a history of more frequent hospitalizations, and the presence of other problems such as suicide gestures and self-mutilation (316, 320). The presence of borderline personality disorder is also associated with poorer treatment outcome and higher levels of psychopathology at follow up (321, 322). Although it has not yet been systematically studied, clinical consensus strongly suggests that the presence of a comorbid personality disorder, particularly borderline personality disorder, dictates the need for longer-term therapy that focuses on the underlying personality structure and dealing with interpersonal relationships in addition to the symptoms of the eating disorder.

4. Posttraumatic stress disorder (PTSD)

Available data on the extent of PTSD among patients with eating disorders are still limited. According to one national survey (323), the lifetime rate of PTSD was nearly 37% among women with bulimia nervosa, much higher than the rate of PTSD seen in community cohorts. There are higher rates of abuse history in patients with bulimia nervosa. Histories of trauma and PTSD are likely to be important in therapy and should be taken into consideration.

▶ C. CONCURRENT GENERAL MEDICAL CONDITIONS

1. Type 1 diabetes mellitus

Eating disorder symptoms appear to be more common among females with diabetes mellitus than in the general population. Thus, a high index of suspicion for these disorders is warranted for those working with young female diabetic patients. The presentation of eating disorders in the context of diabetes mellitus may be substantially more complex than that seen with eating disorders alone, may require more interaction with general medical specialists, and may present as numerous general medical crises before the presence of the eating disorder is diagnosed and treated. There is good evidence that when bulimia nervosa or eating disorder not otherwise specified co-occur with diabetes mellitus, rates of diabetic complications are higher. Diabetics with eating disorders often underdose their insulin in order to lose weight. Out-of-control diabetics with bulimia nervosa may require a period of inpatient treatment for stabilization of both the diabetes mellitus and the disturbed eating (324, 325).

Parenthetically, poor compliance or underdosing with weight-inducing medications such as steroids, anticonvulsants, lithium, and other psychotropic medications necessary for the treatment of other conditions occurs often in patients with eating disorders and even in those with subclinical weight concerns.

2. Pregnancy

Eating disorders may begin de novo during pregnancy, but many patients get pregnant even while they are actively symptomatic with an eating disorder. The behaviors associated with eating disorders including inadequate nutritional intake, binge eating, purging by various means, and the use or abuse of some teratogenic medications (e.g., to varying degrees lithium, benzodiazepines, or divalproex) can all result in fetal or maternal complications (326).

The care of a pregnant patient with an eating disorder is difficult and usually requires the collaboration of a psychiatrist and an obstetrician who specializes in high-risk pregnancies (327–330). Although some patients may be able to eat normally and decrease binge eating and purging during their pregnancy, it is best for the eating disorder to be treated before the pregnancy if possible. Among patients whose symptoms abate during pregnancy, there is some evidence that the eating disorder symptoms often recur after delivery (331). Although women with lifetime histories of anorexia nervosa may not have reduced fertility, they do appear to be at risk of a greater number of birth complications than comparison subjects and of giving birth to babies of lower birth weight (304). This is true both for women who are actively anorectic at the time of pregnancy as well as for women with a prior history of anorexia nervosa. Mothers with eating disorders may have more difficulties than others in feeding their babies and young children than other mothers and may need additional guidance, assistance, and monitoring of their mothering (170–172).

D. DEMOGRAPHIC VARIABLES

1. Male gender

Especially in bulimia subgroups, males with eating disorders who present to tertiary care centers may have more comorbid substance use disorders and more antisocial personality disorders than females. Like females, they are prone to osteoporosis (332). Although gender does not appear to influence the outcome of treatment, some aspects of treatment may need to be modified on the basis of gender. Open-blind studies suggest that normalizing testosterone in males during nutritional rehabilitation for anorexia nervosa may be helpful in increasing lean muscle mass, but definitive studies are not completed. Although studies in clinical samples have suggested that there might be a higher incidence of homosexuality among males with eating disorders (333, 334), this has not yet been confirmed epidemiologically. Nevertheless, since issues concerning sexual orientation are not uncommon among males with eating disorders seen in clinical settings, these issues should be considered in treatment (333). Where possible, therapy groups for males alone may address some of the specific needs of these patients and help them deal with the occasional stigmatization of males by females in treatment. Males with anorexia nervosa may require higher energy intakes (up to 4,000–4,500 kcal/day), since they normally have higher lean body mass and lower fat mass compared to females. And, since they are larger to begin with, males with anorexia nervosa often require much larger weight gains to get back to normal weight (335).

Of note, epidemiological prevalence studies of anorexia nervosa and bulimia nervosa indicate that in North America there are probably more males with bulimia nervosa than females with anorexia nervosa. Although eating disorders are much more prevalent in women, males with eating disorders are not rare and case series of males often report on hundreds of patients (333, 335). The stereotype that eating disorders are female illnesses may limit a full understanding of the scope and nature of problems faced by male patients with eating disorders.

2. Age

Although most eating disorders start while patients are in their teens and 20s, earlier and later onsets are encountered as well. In some patients with early onsets (i.e., between ages 7 and 12), obsessional behavior and depression are common. Children often present with physical symptoms such as nausea, abdominal pain, feeling full, or being unable to swallow; their weight loss can be rapid and dramatic. Children with early-onset anorexia nervosa may suffer from delayed growth (174, 336–340) and may be especially prone to osteopenia and osteoporosis (51, 52). In a few cases, exacerbations of anorexia nervosa and OCD-like symptoms have been associated with pediatric infection-triggered autoimmune neuropsychiatric disorders (341, 342). Bulimia nervosa under the age of 12 is rare.

Anorexia nervosa has been reported in elderly patients in their 70s and 80s, in whom the illness has generally been present for 40 or 50 years. In many cases the illness started after age 25 (so-called anorexia tardive). In some case reports, adverse life events such as deaths, marital crisis, or divorce have been found to trigger these older-onset syndromes. Fear of aging has also been described as a major precipitating factor in some patients (19, 343). Rates of comorbid depression have been reported to be higher among these patients in some studies but not in others (344).

3. Cultural factors

Specific pressures and values concerning weight and shape vary among different cultures. Strivings for beauty and acceptance according to the stereotypes they perceive in global-cast media are leading increasing numbers of women around the world to develop attitudes and eating behaviors associated with eating disorders (105, 345). Clinicians should engage these women in informed and sensitive discussions regarding their struggles and personal experiences about what it means to be feminine and what it means to be "perfect" in the modern world (346). Clinicians should be sensitive to and inquire as to how weight and shape concerns are experienced by patients, especially those who are minorities, from non-Western or other cultural backgrounds, or are transitioning and assimilating into Western societies.

4. Eating disorders in athletes

Eating disorders are more common among competitive athletes than the general age-matched population (347, 348). Female athletes are especially at risk in sports that emphasize a thin body or appearance, such as gymnastics, ballet, figure skating, and distance running. Males in sports such as bodybuilding and wrestling are also at greater risk. Certain antecedent factors such as cultural preoccupation with thinness, performance anxiety, and athlete self-appraisal may predispose a female athlete to body dissatisfaction, which often mediates the development of eating disorder symptoms (349). Parents and coaches of young athletes may support distorted shape and eating attitudes in the service of guiding the athlete to be more competitive.

Physicians working with adolescent and young adult athletes, particularly those athletes participating in the at-risk sports, must be alert to early symptoms of eating disorders. Simple screening questions about weight, possible dissatisfaction with appearance, amenorrhea, and nutritional intake on the day before evaluation may help identify an athlete who is developing an eating disorder. Early general medical and psychiatric intervention is key to prompt recovery.

Extreme exercise appears to be a risk factor for developing anorexia nervosa, especially when combined with dieting (112). A "female athlete triad" has been identified, consisting of disordered eating, amenorrhea, and osteoporosis (350). Similarly, an "overtraining syndrome" has been described: a state of exhaustion, depression, and irritability in which athletes continue to train but their performance diminishes (351). Both have been linked to the syndrome of "activity anorexia," which has been observed in animal models (352).

5. Eating disorders in high schools and colleges

Eating disorders are common among female high school and college students, and psychiatrists and other health and mental health professionals may be involved in their care in various ways. From a primary prevention perspective, health professionals may be called upon to provide information and education about eating disorders in classrooms, athletic programs, and assorted other extracurricular venues. The efficacy of such programs for the reduction of eating disorders is still uncertain (353, 354). Helping in early intervention, health professionals may serve as trainers, coordinators, and professional supports for peer counseling efforts conducted at school, in dormitories, and through other campus institutions. Through student health and student psychological services, they may serve as initial screeners and diagnosticians and help manage students with varying levels of severity of eating disorders (355).

On occasion psychiatrists may be called upon as clinicians and as agents of the school administration to offer guidance in the management of impaired students with serious eating disorders. In such situations the suggested guidelines for levels of care described in table 1 should be followed. Accordingly, to stay in school students must be treatable as outpatients. It is advisable that students be required to take a leave of absence if they are severely ill (355, 356). The student should be directed to inpatient hospital care if weight is 30% or more below an expected healthy weight, or if any of the other indications for hospitalization listed in table 1 are present.

For students with serious eating disorders who remain in school, the psychiatrist and other health providers should work with the school's administration toward developing policies and programs that make student attendance contingent upon participation in a suitable treatment program. For the severely ill student, the clinical team must include a general medical clinician who can gauge safety and monitor weight, vital signs, and laboratory indicators. For the student to be permitted to continue in school, these clinicians may require a minimum weight and other physical, behavioral, or laboratory target measures to ensure basic medical safety. An explicit policy should be developed specifying that clinicians have the final say regarding the student's participation in physically demanding activities such as organized athletics. Restrictions must be based on actual medical concerns. Procedures should be in compliance with the school's policies regarding management of students with psychiatric disabilities and the Americans with Disabilities Act (356).

VI. RESEARCH DIRECTIONS

Further studies of eating disorders are needed that address issues surrounding the epidemiology, causes, and course of illness. Areas of specific concern include:

1. Genetic and other biological, gender-related, psychological, familial, social, and cultural risk factors that contribute to the development of specific eating disorders, greater morbidity and higher mortality, treatment resistance, and risk of relapse.
2. Structure-function relationships associated with predisposing vulnerabilities, nutritional changes associated with the disorders, and changes in recovery examined through imaging studies.
3. The differential presentation of eating disorders across various developmental periods from early childhood through late adulthood.
4. Linkages between physiological and psychological processes of puberty and the onset of typical eating disorders.
5. The impact of various comorbid conditions (including mood, anxiety, substance abuse, obsessive-compulsive symptoms, personality disorders, PTSD, cognitive impairments, and other commonly encountered concurrent disorders) on course and treatment response.
6. The effect of exercise, including the role of extreme exercise, and food restriction in precipitating and maintaining eating disorders. Conversely, the possible protective effect of contemporary women's athletics on girls' eating and weight attitudes.
7. Further delineation and definition of eating disorder not otherwise specified and binge-eating disorder, with clarification of risk factors, morbidity, treatments, and prognosis.
8. Family studies on factors associated with onset and maintenance of eating disorders, as well as concerning the impact of eating disorders on other family members.
9. Culturally flexible diagnostic criteria to allow for the identification and treatment of the many "atypical" cases, which may represent a large number of eating disorders patients in non-Western societies.

Additional studies and assessments of new interventions are also needed, specifically with regard to

1. Primary prevention programs in schools and through the media.
2. Targeted prevention through screenings and risk-factor early intervention programs.
3. Improved guidelines for choice of treatment setting and selection of specific treatments on the basis of more refined clinical indicators and a better understanding of the stages of these disorders (including follow-up issues for short-term and long-term treatment studies).

4. Development and testing of newer biological agents affecting hunger, satiety, and energy expenditure as well as commonly associated psychiatric symptoms and conditions.
5. Development and testing of various individually administered and "bundled" individual and group psychotherapies including cognitive behavior, interpersonal, psychodynamic, psychoanalytic, and family therapies as well as nutritional therapies and other psychosocial therapies (creative arts, 12-step models, and professional or layperson-led support groups and self-help groups for patients and families).
6. Treatment outcome studies related to various systems or settings of care, including HMO versus fee for service; limitations of hospital or other intensive treatment resources due to managed care and other resource limitations; treatment in eating disorder specialty units versus general psychiatry treatment units; and impact of staff composition, professional background of providers, system or setting characteristics, and roles of primary care versus mental health providers in the treatment of eating disorders.
7. Further development and testing of professionally designed self-administered treatments by manuals and computer-based treatment programs.
8. Modifications of treatment required because of various comorbid conditions.
9. The impact of commonly used "alternative" and "complementary" therapies on the course of illness.
10. New methods for assessing and treating osteopenia, osteoporosis, and other long-term medical sequelae.
11. Further delineation of proper education and training for psychiatrists and other healthcare providers to deal with patients with eating disorders.

VII. INDIVIDUALS AND ORGANIZATIONS THAT SUBMITTED COMMENTS

Carl Bell, M.D.
Peter J. V. Beumont, M.D.
Cynthia Bulik, M.D.
Paula Clayton, M.D.
Scott Crow, M.D.
Dave M. Davis, M.D.
David R. DeMaso, M.D.
Judith Dogin, M.D.
Christopher G. Fairburn, Ph.D.
Aaron H. Fink, M.D.
Martin Fisher, M.D.
Sara Forman, M.D.
David M. Garner, M.D.
Neville H. Golden, M.D.
Joseph Hagan, M.D.
Allan S. Kaplan, M.D.
Debra K. Katzman, M.D.
Melanie A. Katzman, M.D.
Diane Keddy, M.S., R.D.

Thomas E. Kottke, M.D., M.S.P.H.
Richard Kreipe, M.D.
Elaine Lonegran, M.S.W., Ph.D.
Jerome A. Motto, M.D.
Diane Mickley, M.D.
Jean Bradley Rubel, Ph.D.
Marian Schienholtz, M.S.W.
Paul M. Schyve, M.D.
Reba Sloan, M.P.H., L.R.D.
Mae Sokol, M.D.
Joshua Sparrow, M.D.
Michael Strober, M.D.
Albert Stunkard, M.D.
Richard T. Suchinsky, M.D.
Jack Swanson, M.D.
Janet Treasure, M.D.
Joe Westermeyer, M.D.
Denise Wilfley, Ph.D.
Stephen Wonderlich, Ph.D.

American Academy of Pediatrics
American Association of Directors of Psychiatric Residency Training
American Association of Suicidology
American Dietetic Association (Sports, Cardiovascular and Wellness Nutritionists)
Anorexia Nervosa and Related Eating Disorders
American Group Psychotherapy Association
Black Psychiatrists of America
Center for Eating and Weight Disorders
Joint Commission on Accreditation of Health Care Organizations

VIII. REFERENCES

∎∎

The following coding system is used to indicate the nature of the supporting evidence in the references:

[A] *Randomized clinical trial.* A study of an intervention in which subjects are prospectively followed over time; there are treatment and control groups; subjects are randomly assigned to the two groups; both the subjects and the investigators are blind to the assignments.

[B] *Clinical trial.* A prospective study in which an intervention is made and the results of that intervention are tracked longitudinally; study does not meet standards for a randomized clinical trial.

[C] *Cohort or longitudinal study.* A study in which subjects are prospectively followed over time without any specific intervention.

[D] *Case-control study.* A study in which a group of patients and a group of control subjects are identified in the present and information about them is pursued retrospectively or backward in time.

[E] *Review with secondary analysis.* A structured analytic review of existing data, e.g., a meta-analysis or a decision analysis.

[F] *Review.* A qualitative review and discussion of previously published literature without a quantitative synthesis of the data.

[G] *Other.* Textbooks, expert opinion, case reports, and other reports not included above.

1. LaVia M, Kaye WH, Andersen A, Bowers W, Brandt HA, Brewerton TD, Costin C, Hill L, Lilenfeld L, McGilley B, Powers PS, Pryor T, Yager J, Zucker ML: Anorexia nervosa: criteria for levels of care. Eating Disorders Research Society Annual Meeting, Boston, 1998 [G]
2. Crisp AH, Callender JS, Halek C, Hsu LK: Long-term mortality in anorexia nervosa: a 20-year follow-up of the St George's and Aberdeen cohorts. Br J Psychiatry 1992; 161:104–107 [C]
3. Appelbaum PS, Rumpf T: Civil commitment of the anorexic patient. Gen Hosp Psychiatry 1998; 20:225–230 [G]
4. Maxmen JS, Silberfarb PM, Ferrell RB: Anorexia nervosa: practical initial management in a general hospital. JAMA 1974; 229:801–803 [G]
5. Treasure J, Palmer RL: Providing specialized services for anorexia nervosa. Br J Psychiatry (in press) [D]
6. Kaye W, Kaplan AS, Zucker ML: Treating eating disorders in a managed care environment. Psychiatr Clin North Am 1996; 19:793–810 [F]
7. Kaplan AS, Olmsted MP: Partial hospitalization, in Handbook of Treatment for Eating Disorders, 2nd ed. Edited by Garner DM, Garfinkel PE. New York, Guilford Press, 1997, pp 354–360 [G]
8. American Psychiatric Association: Practice guideline for eating disorders. Am J Psychiatry 1993; 150:212–228 [I]
9. Andersen AE: Practical Comprehensive Treatment of Anorexia Nervosa and Bulimia. Baltimore, Md, Johns Hopkins University Press, 1985 [I]
10. Owen W, Halmi KA: Medical evaluation and management of anorexia nervosa, in Treatments of Psychiatric Disorders: A Task Force Report of the American Psychiatric Association, vol 1. Washington, DC, APA, 1989, pp 517–519 [I]

11. Kaplan AS, Garfinkel P: Difficulties in treating patients with eating disorders: a review of patient and clinician variables. Can J Psychiatry 1999 (in press) [G]

12. Wooley SC: Uses of countertransference in the treatment of eating disorders: a gender perspective, in Psychodynamic Treatment of Anorexia Nervosa and Bulimia. Edited by Johnson CL. New York, Guilford Press, 1991, pp 245–294 [G]

13. Zerbe KJ: Knowable secrets: transference and countertransference manifestations in eating disordered patients, in Treating Eating Disorders: Ethical, Legal, and Personal Issues. Edited by Vandereycken W, Beumont PJV. New York, New York University Press, 1998, pp 30–55 [G]

14. Zunino N, Agoos E, Davis WN: The impact of therapist gender on the treatment of bulimic women. Int J Eat Disord 1991; 10:253–263 [E]

15. Katzman MA, Waller G: Implications of therapist gender in the treatment of eating disorders: daring to ask the questions, in The Burden of the Therapist. Edited by Vandereycken W. London, Athelone Press, 1998, pp 56–79 [G]

16. Waller G, Katzman MA: Female or male therapists for women with eating disorders? a pilot study of expert opinions. Int J Eat Disord 1997; 22:111–114 [G]

17. Bloom C, Gitter A, Gutwill S: Eating Problems: A Feminist Psychoanalytic Treatment Model. New York, Basic Books, 1994 [G]

18. Zerbe KJ: The Body Betrayed: Women, Eating Disorders, and Treatment. Washington, DC, American Psychiatric Press, 1993 [G]

19. Zerbe KJ: Whose body is it anyway? understanding and treating psychosomatic aspects of eating disorders. Bull Menninger Clin 1993; 57:161–177 [F]

20. Werne J: Treating Eating Disorders. San Francisco, Jossey-Bass, 1996 [G]

21. Yager J: Patients with chronic, recalcitrant eating disorders, in Special Problems in Managing Eating Disorders. Edited by Yager J, Gwirtsman HE, Edelstein CK. Washington, DC, American Psychiatric Press, 1992, pp 205–231 [G]

22. Zerbe KJ: Integrating feminist and psychodynamic principles in the treatment of an eating disorder patient: implications for using countertransference responses. Bull Menninger Clin 1995; 59:160–176 [G]

23. Kaplan AS, Fallon P: Therapeutic boundaries in the treatment of patients with eating disorders. Fourth London International Conference on Eating Disorders, April 20–22, 1999, p 30 [G]

24. Andersen AE: Hospital Treatment of Anorexia Nervosa. Washington, DC, American Psychiatric Press, 1989 [I]

25. Kaplan AS: Medical and nutritional assessment, in Medical Issues and the Eating Disorders: The Interface. Edited by Kaplan AS, Garfinkel PE. New York, Brunner/Mazel, 1993, pp 1–16 [G]

26. Powers PS: Initial assessment and early treatment options for anorexia nervosa and bulimia nervosa. Psychiatr Clin North Am 1996; 19:639–655 [F]

27. Strober M, Freeman R, Morrell W: The long-term course of severe anorexia nervosa in adolescents: survival analysis of recovery, relapse, and outcome predictors over 10–15 years in a prospective study. Int J Eat Disord 1997; 22:339–360 [C]

28. Bulik C, Sullivan PF, Fear J, Pickering A: Predictors of the development of bulimia nervosa in women with anorexia nervosa. J Nerv Ment Dis 1997; 185:704–707 [G]

29. Lee S, Ho TP, Hsu LKG: Fat phobic and non-fat phobic anorexia nervosa—a comparative study of 70 Chinese patients in Hong Kong. Psychol Med 1993; 23:999–1004 [D]

30. Strober M, Freeman R, Morrell W: Atypical anorexia nervosa: separation from typical cases in course and outcome in a long-term prospective study. Int J Eat Disord 1999; 25:135–142 [C]

31. Beumont PJ, George GC, Smart DE: Dieters and vomiters and purgers in anorexia nervosa. Psychol Med 1976; 6:617–622 [C]

32. Casper RC, Eckert ED, Halmi KA, Goldberg SC, Davis JM: Bulimia: its incidence and clinical importance in patients with anorexia nervosa. Arch Gen Psychiatry 1980; 37:1030–1035 [C]

33. Garfinkel PE, Moldofsky H, Garner DM: The heterogeneity of anorexia nervosa: bulimia as a distinct group. Arch Gen Psychiatry 1980; 37:1036–1040 [C]

34. Kassett JA, Gwirtsman HE, Kaye WH, Brandt HA, Jimerson DC: Pattern of onset of bulimic symptoms in anorexia nervosa. Am J Psychiatry 1988; 145:1287–1288 [C]

35. Wilson CP, Hogan CC, Mintz IL: Fear of Being Fat: The Treatment Of Anorexia Nervosa and Bulimia, 2nd ed. Northvale, NJ, Jason Aronson, 1985 [F]

36. Wilson CP, Hogan CC, Mintz IL: Psychodynamic Technique in the Treatment of Eating Disorders. Northvale, NJ, Jason Aronson, 1992 [F]

37. Bunnell DW, Shenker IR, Nussbaum MP, Jacobson MS, Cooper P, Phil D: Subclinical versus formal eating disorders: differentiating psychological features. Int J Eat Disord 1990; 9:357–362 [D]

38. Zerbe KJ: The emerging sexual self of the patient with an eating disorder: implications for treatment. Eating Disorders: J Treatment and Prevention 1995; 3:197–215 [B]

39. Favazza AR, DeRosear L, Conterio K: Self-mutilation and eating disorders. Suicide Life Threat Behav 1989; 19:352–361 [G]

40. Johnson C, Connors ME: The Etiology and Treatment of Bulimia Nervosa. New York, Basic Books, 1987 [I]

41. Rizzuto A: Transference, language, and affect in the treatment of bulimarexia. Int J Psychoanal 1988; 69:369–387 [G]

42. Schwartz HJ: Bulimia: Psychoanalytic Treatment and Theory, 2nd ed. Madison, Conn, International Universities Press, 1990 [I]

43. Lacey H: Bulimia nervosa, binge-eating, and psychogenic vomiting: a controlled treatment study and long-term outcome. Br Med J 1983; 2:1609–1613 [A]

44. Casper RC, Davis JM: On the course of anorexia nervosa. Am J Psychiatry 1977; 134:974–978 [C]

45. Garfinkel PE, Kaplan AS: Starvation based perpetuating mechanisms in anorexia nervosa and bulimia. Int J Eat Disord 1985; 4:651–655 [E]

46. Keys A, Brozek J, Henschel A, Mickelsen O, Taylor HL: The Biology of Human Starvation. Minneapolis, University of Minnesota Press, 1950 [B]

47. Srinivasagam NM, Kaye WH, Plotnicov KH, Greeno C, Weltzin TE, Rao R: Persistent perfectionism, symmetry, and exactness after long-term recovery from anorexia nervosa. Am J Psychiatry 1995; 152:1630–1634 [C]

48. Garner DM, Garfinkel PE (eds): Handbook of Psychotherapy for Anorexia Nervosa and Bulimia. New York, Guilford Press, 1985 [G]

49. Fichter MM: Starvation-related endocrine changes, in Psychobiology and Treatment of Anorexia Nervosa and Bulimia Nervosa. Edited by Halmi KA. Washington, DC, American Psychopathological Association, 1992, pp 193–210 [G]

50. Fichter MM, Pirke KM, Pollinger J, Wolfram G, Brunner E: Disturbances in the hypothalamo-pituitary-adrenal and other neuroendocrine axes in bulimia. Biol Psychiatry 1990; 27:1021–1037 [D]

51. Bachrach LK, Guido D, Katzman DK, Litt IF, Marcus RN: Decreased bone density in adolescent girls with anorexia nervosa. Pediatrics 1990; 86:440–447 [C]

52. Bachrach LK, Katzman DK, Litt IF, Guido D, Marcus RN: Recovery from osteopenia in adolescent girls with anorexia nervosa. J Clin Endocrinol Metab 1991; 72:602–606 [B]

53. Rigotti NA, Neer RM, Skates SJ, Herzog DB, Nussbaum SR: The clinical course of osteoporosis in anorexia nervosa: a longitudinal study of cortical bone mass. JAMA 1991; 265:1133–1138 [B]

54. Klibanski A, Biller BM, Schoenfeld DA, Herzog DB, Saxe VC: The effects of estrogen administration on trabecular bone loss in young women with anorexia nervosa. J Clin Endocrinol Metab 1995; 80:898–904 [B]

55. Stewart DE, Robinson E, Goldbloom DS, Wright C: Infertility and eating disorders. Am J Obstet Gynecol 1990; 163:1196–1199 [C]

56. Beumont PJV, Kopec-Schrader EM, Lennerts W: Eating disorder patients at a NSW teaching hospital: a comparison with state-wide data. Aust NZ J Psychiatry 1995; 29:96–103 [G]

57. de Zwaan M, Mitchell JE: Medical complications of anorexia nervosa and bulimia nervosa, in Medical Issues and the Eating Disorders: The Interface. Edited by Kaplan AS, Garfinkel PE. New York, Brunner/Mazel, 1993, pp 60–100 [G]

58. Garfinkel PE, Garner DM: The Role of Drug Treatments for Eating Disorders. New York, Brunner/Mazel, 1987 [I]

59. Halmi KA: Anorexia nervosa and bulimia. Annu Rev Med 1987; 38:373–380 [F]

60. Herzog DB, Copeland PM: Eating disorders. N Engl J Med 1985; 313:295–303 [F]

61. Krieg JC, Pirke KM, Lauer C, Backmund H: Endocrine, metabolic, and cranial computed tomographic findings in anorexia nervosa. Biol Psychiatry 1988; 23:377–387 [G]

62. Golden NH, Ashtari M, Kohn MR, Patel M, Jacobson MS, Fletcher A, Shenker IR: Reversibility of cerebral ventricular enlargement in anorexia nervosa demonstrated by quantitative magnetic resonance imaging. J Pediatr 1996; 128:296–301 [B]

63. Katzman DK, Lambe EK, Mikulis DJ, Ridgley JN, Goldbloom DS, Zipursky RB: Cerebral gray matter and white matter volume deficits in adolescent girls with anorexia nervosa. J Pediatr 1996; 129:794–803 [D]

64. Kingston K, Szmukler G, Andrewes D, Tress B, Desmond P: Neuropsychological and structural brain changes in anorexia nervosa before and after refeeding. Psychol Med 1996; 26:15–28 [C]

65. Lambe EK, Katzman DK, Mikulis DJ, Kennedy S, Zipursky RB: Cerebral gray matter volume deficits after weight recovery from anorexia nervosa. Arch Gen Psychiatry 1997; 54:537–542 [C]

66. Swayze VW II, Andersen A, Arndt S, Rajarethinam R, Fleming F, Sato Y, Andreasen NC: Reversibility of brain tissue loss in anorexia nervosa assessed with a computerized Talairach 3-D proportional grid. Psychol Med 1996; 26:381–390 [C]

67. Hamsher K, Halmi KA, Benton AL: Prediction of outcome in anorexia nervosa from neuropsychological status. Psychiatry Res 1981; 4:79–88 [C]

68. Powers PS, Tyson IB, Stevens BA, Heal AV: Total body potassium and serum potassium among eating disorder patients. Int J Eat Disord 1995; 18:269–276 [G]

69. Mitchell JE, Pyle RL, Eckert ED, Hatsukami D, Lentz R: Electrolyte and other physiological abnormalities in patients with bulimia. Psychol Med 1983; 13:273–278 [G]

70. Herzog DB, Nussbaum KM, Marmor AK: Comorbidity and outcome in eating disorders. Psychiatr Clin North Am 1996; 19:843–859 [F]

71. Halmi KA, Eckert E, Marchi P, Sampugnaro V, Apple R, Cohen J: Comorbidity of psychiatric diagnoses in anorexia nervosa. Arch Gen Psychiatry 1991; 48:712–718 [C]

72. Theander S: Outcome and prognosis in anorexia nervosa and bulimia: some results of previous investigations compared with those of a Swedish long term study. J Psychiatr Res 1985; 19:493–508 [C]

73. Sullivan PF: Mortality in anorexia nervosa. Am J Psychiatry 1995; 152:1073–1074 [E]

74. Harris EC, Barraclough B: Excess mortality of mental disorder. Br J Psychiatry 1998; 173:11–53 [F]

75. Hsu LKG: Outcome and treatment effects, in Handbook of Eating Disorders. Edited by Beaumont PJV, Burrows BD, Casper RC. Amsterdam, Elsevier, 1987, pp 371–377 [I]

76. Hsu LKG: Eating Disorders. New York, Guilford Press, 1990 [I]

77. Russell G: Bulimia nervosa: an ominous variant of anorexia nervosa. Psychol Med 1979; 9:429–488 [E]

78. Kreipe RE, Churchill BH, Strauss J: Long-term outcome of adolescents with anorexia nervosa. Am J Dis Child 1989; 43:1322–1327 [C]

79. Nussbaum MP, Shenker IR, Baird D, Saravay S: Follow up investigation of patients with anorexia nervosa. J Pediatr 1985; 106:835–840 [C]

80. Steiner H, Mazer C, Litt IF: Compliance and outcome in anorexia nervosa. West J Med 1990; 153:133–139 [C]

81. Drewnowski A, Yee DK, Krahn DD: Dieting and Bulimia: A Continuum of Behaviors. Washington, DC, American Psychiatric Press, 1989 [G]

82. Yager J, Landsverk J, Edelstein CK: A 20-month follow-up study of 628 women with eating disorders, I: course and severity. Am J Psychiatry 1987; 144:1172–1177 [B]

83. Hsu LK, Sobkiewicz TA: Bulimia nervosa: a four to six year follow up. Psychol Med 1989; 19:1035–1038 [B]

84. Keel PK, Mitchell JE: Outcome in bulimia nervosa. Am J Psychiatry 1997; 154:313–321 [F]

85. Keel PK, Mitchell JE, Miller KB, Davis TL, Crow SJ: Long-term outcome of bulimia nervosa. Arch Gen Psychiatry 1998; 56:63–69 [E]

86. Luka LP, Agras WS, Schneider JA: Thirty month follow up of cognitive behavioral group therapy for bulimia (letter). Br J Psychiatry 1986; 148:614–615 [B]

87. Fichter MM, Quadflieg N: Six-year course of bulimia nervosa. Int J Eat Disord 1997; 22:361–384 [C]

88. Swift WJ, Ritholz M, Kalin NH, Kaslow N: A follow-up study of thirty hospitalized bulimics. Psychosom Med 1987; 49:45–55 [B]

89. Agras WS, Walsh T, Wilson G: A multisite comparison of cognitive behavior therapy (CBT) and interpersonal therapy (IPT) in the treatment of bulimia nervosa. Fourth London International Conference on Eating Disorders, April 20–22, 1999, p 61 [G]

90. Olmsted MP, Kaplan AS, Rockert W: Rate and prediction of relapse in bulimia nervosa. Am J Psychiatry 1994; 151:738–743 [C]

91. Garfinkel PE, Lin E, Goering P, Spegg C, Goldbloom D, Kennedy S, Kaplan AS, Woodside DB: Should amenorrhoea be necessary for the diagnosis of anorexia nervosa. Br J Psychiatry 1996; 168:500–506 [G]

92. Walters EE, Kendler KS: Anorexia nervosa and anorexic-like syndromes in a population-based female twin sample. Am J Psychiatry 1995; 152:64–71 [D]

93. Garfinkel PE, Lin E, Goering P, Spegg C, Goldbloom DS, Kennedy S, Kaplan AS, Woodside DB: Bulimia nervosa in a Canadian community sample: prevalence and comparison of subgroups. Am J Psychiatry 1995; 152:1052–1058 [C]

94. Kendler KS, MacLean C, Neale M, Kessler R, Heath A, Eaves L: The genetic epidemiology of bulimia nervosa. Am J Psychiatry 1991; 148:1627–1637 [H]

95. Heatherton TF, Nichols P, Mahamedi F, Keel P: Body weight, dieting, and eating disorder symptoms among college students, 1982 to 1992. Am J Psychiatry 1995; 152:1623–1629 [D]

96. Fosson A, Knibbs J, Bryant-Waugh R, Lask B: Early onset of anorexia nervosa. Arch Dis Childhood 1987; 62:114–118 [F]

97. Hawley RM: The outcome of anorexia nervosa in younger subjects. Br J Psychiatry 1985; 146:657–660 [C]

98. Higgs JF, Goodyer IN, Birch J: Anorexia nervosa and food avoidance emotional disorder. Arch Dis Childhood 1989; 64:346–351 [D]

99. Pate JE, Pumariega AJ, Hester C, Garner DM: Cross cultural patterns in eating disorders: a review. Am J Child Adolesc Psychiatry 1992; 31:802–809 [F]

100. Kiriike N, Nagata T, Tanaka M, Nishiwaki S, Takeuchi N, Kawakita Y: Prevalence of binge-eating and bulimia among adolescent women in Japan. Psychiatry Res 1988; 26:163–169 [D]

101. Nadaoka T, Oiji A, Takahashi S, Morioka Y, Kashiwakura M, Totsuka S: An epidemiological study of eating disorders in a northern area of Japan. Acta Psychiatr Scand 1996; 93:305–310 [D]

102. Davis C, Katzman MA: Chinese men and women in the USA and Hong Kong: body and self-esteem ratings as a prelude to dieting and exercise. Int J Eat Disord 1998; 23:99–102 [D]

103. Davis C, Katzman MA: Perfection as acculturation: psychological correlates of eating problems in Chinese male and female students living in the United States. Int J Eat Disord 1999; 25:65–70 [D]

104. Becker AE: Acculturation and Disordered Eating in Fiji. Washington, DC, American Psychiatric Press, 1999 [G]

105. Nasser M: Culture and Weight Consciousness. New York, Routledge, 1997 [G]

106. Toro J, Cervera M, Perez P: Body shape, publicity and anorexia nervosa. Social Psychiatry Psychiatr Epidemiol 1988; 23:132–136 [E]

107. Toro J, Nicolau R, Cervera M, Castro J, Blecua MJ, Zaragoza M, Toro A: A clinical and phenomenological study of 185 Spanish adolescents with anorexia nervosa. Eur Child Adolesc Psychiatry 1995; 4:165–174 [E]

108. Crago M, Shisslak CM, Estes LS: Eating disturbances among American minority groups: a review. Int J Eat Disord 1996; 19:239–248 [F]

109. Langer L, Warheit G, Zimmerman R: Epidemiological study of problem eating behaviors and related attitudes in the general population. Addict Behav 1992; 16:167–173 [D]

110. Warheit G, Langer L, Zimmerman R, Biafora F: Prevalence of bulimic behaviors and bulimia among a sample of the general population. Am J Epidemiol 1993; 137:569–576 [D]

111. Pumariega AJ, Gustavson CR, Gustavson JC: Eating attitudes in African-American women: the essence. Eating Disorders: J Treatment and Prevention 1994; 2:5–16 [D]

112. Davis C, Kennedy SH, Ravelski E, Dionne M: The role of physical activity in the development and maintenance of eating disorders. Psychol Med 1994; 24:957–967 [B]

113. Garner DM, Rosen LW, Barry D: Eating disorders among athletes: research and recommendations. Child Adolesc Psychiatr Clin North Am 1998; 7:839–857 [F]

114. Strober M, Lampert C, Morrell W, Burroughs J, Jacobs C: a controlled family study of anorexia nervosa: evidence of familial aggregation and lack of shared transmission with affective disorders. Int J Eat Disord 1990; 9:239–253 [B]

115. Bulik C, Sullivan P, Carter FA, McIntosh VV, Joyce PR: The role of exposure with response prevention in the cognitive behavioral therapy for bulimia nervosa. Psychol Med 1998; 28:611–623 [B]

116. Lilenfeld L, Kaye W, Greeno C, Merikangas KR, Plotnicov KH, Pollice C, Radhika R, Strober M, Bulik C, Nagy L: Psychiatric disorders in women with bulimia nervosa and their first-degree relatives: effects of comorbid substance dependence. Int J Eat Disord 1997; 22:253–264 [D]

117. Mitchell JE, Hatsukami D, Pyle R, Eckert E: Bulimia with and without a family history of drug use. Addict Behav 1988; 13:245–251 [C]

118. Hudson JI, Pope HG Jr, Yurgelun-Todd D, Jonas JM, Frankenburg FR: A controlled study of lifetime prevalence of affective and other psychiatric disorders in bulimic outpatients. Am J Psychiatry 1987; 144:1283–1287 [C]

119. Pyle RL, Mitchell JE, Eckert ED: Bulimia: a report of 34 cases. J Clin Psychiatry 1981; 42:60–64 [G]

120. Zerbe KJ: Feminist psychodynamic psychotherapy of eating disorders: theoretic integration informing clinical practice. Psychiatr Clin North Am 1996; 19:811–827 [F]

121. Zerbe KJ, March S, Coyne L: Comorbidity in an inpatient eating disorders population: clinical characteristics and treatment implications. Psychiatr Hospital 1993; 24:3–8 [D]

122. Braun DL, Sunday SR, Halmi KA: Psychiatric comorbidity in patients with eating disorders. Psychol Med 1994; 24:859–867 [C]

123. Herzog DB, Keller MB, Sacks NR, Yeh CJ, Lavori PW: Psychiatric comorbidity in treatment-seeking anorexics and bulimics. J Am Acad Child Adolesc Psychiatry 1992; 31:810–818 [D]

124. Hudson JI, Pope HG, Jonas JM, Yurgelun-Todd D: Phenomenologic relationship of eating disorders to major affective disorder. Psychiatry Res 1983; 9:345–354 [D]

125. Hecht H, Fichter MM, Postpeschil F: Obsessive-compulsive neuroses and anorexia nervosa. Int J Eat Disord 1983; 2:69–77 [D]

126. Kasvikis YG, Tsakiris F, Marks IM, Basogul M, Noshirvani HF: Past history of anorexia nervosa in women with obsessive compulsive disorder. Int J Eat Disord 1986; 5:1069–1076 [C]

127. Skodol AE, Oldham JM, Hyler SE, Kellman HD, Doidge N, Davies M: Comorbidity of DSM-III-R eating disorders and personality disorders. Int J Eat Disord 1993; 14:403–416 [D]

128. Herzog DB, Keller MB, Lavori PW, Kenny GM, Sacks NR: The prevalence of personality disorders in 210 women with eating disorders. J Clin Psychiatry 1992; 53:147–152 [G]

129. Bulik CM, Sullivan PF, Rorty M: Childhood sexual abuse in women with bulimia. J Clin Psychiatry 1989; 50:460–464 [C]

130. Schmidt U, Tiller J, Treasure J: Self-treatment of bulimia nervosa: a pilot study. Int J Eat Disord 1993; 13:273–277 [B]

131. Vize CM, Cooper PJ: Sexual abuse in patients with eating disorder patients with depression and normal controls: a comparative study. Br J Psychiatry 1995; 167:80–85 [D]

132. Pope HG Jr, Hudson JI: Is childhood sexual abuse a risk factor for bulimia nervosa? Am J Psychiatry 1992; 149:455–463 [E]

133. Rorty M, Yager J, Rossotto E: Childhood sexual physical and psychological abuse and their relationship to comorbid psychopathology in bulimia nervosa. Int J Eat Disord 1994; 16:317–334 [C]

134. Wonderlich SA, Brewerton TD, Jocic Z, Dansky BS, Abbott DW: Relationship of childhood sexual abuse and eating disorders. J Am Acad Child Adolesc Psychiatry 1997; 36:1107–1115 [F]

135. Wonderlich SA, Mitchell JE: Eating disorders and comorbidity: empirical, conceptual and clinical implications. Psychopharmacol Bull 1997; 33:381–390 [F]

136. Kaye WH, Gwirtsman H, Obarzanek E, George DT: Relative importance of calorie intake needed to gain weight and level of physical activity in anorexia nervosa. Am J Clin Nutr 1988; 47:989–994 [C]

137. Golden NH, Jacobson MS, Schebendach J, Solanto MV, Hertz SM, Shenker IR: Resumption of menses in anorexia nervosa. Arch Pediatr Adolesc Med 1997; 151:16–21 [C]

138. Treasure JL, Wheeler M, King EA, Gordon PA, Russell GF: Weight gain and reproductive function: ultrasonographic and endocrine features in anorexia nervosa. Clin Endocrinol 1988; 29:607–616 [C]

139. Frisch RE: Fatness and fertility. Sci Am 1988; 258:88–95 [F]

140. Metropolitan Life Insurance Company: 1983 Metropolitan height and weight tables. Stat Bull Metrop Life Found 1983; 64:3–9 [E]

141. Hamill PV, Johnston FE, Lemeshow S: Height and weight of youths 12–17 years, United States. Vital Health Stat 1 1973: 11:1–81 [C]

142. Hebebrand J, Himmelmann GW, Heseker H, Schafer H, Remschmidt H: Use of percentiles for the body mass index in anorexia nervosa: diagnostic, epidemiological and therapeutic considerations. Int J Eat Disord 1996; 19:359–369 [D]

143. Reiff DW, Reiff KKL: Set point, in Eating Disorders: Nutrition Therapy in the Recovery Process. Gaithersburg, Md, Aspen, 1992, pp 104–105 [G]

144. Guarda AS, Heinberg LJ: Effective weight-gain in step down partial hospitalization program for eating disorders. Annual Meeting of Academy for Eating Disorders, San Diego, 1999 [G]

145. Powers PS: Heart failure during treatment of anorexia nervosa. Am J Psychiatry 1982; 139:1167–1170 [G]

146. Kohn MR, Golden NH, Shenker IR: Cardiac arrest and delirium: presentations of the refeeding syndrome in severely malnourished adolescents with anorexia nervosa. J Adolesc Health 1998; 22:239–243 [G]

147. Scott M, Solomon, Kriby DF: The refeeding syndrome: a review. JPEN Parenter Enteral Nutr 1990; 14:90–97 [F]

148. Treasure J, Todd G, Szmukler G: The inpatient treatment of anorexia nervosa, in Handbook of Eating Disorders. Edited by Szmukler G, Dare C, Treasure J. Chichester, UK, John Wiley & Sons, 1995, pp 275–291 [G]

149. Kaye WH, Weltzin TE, Hsu LK, Bulik CM: An open trial of fluoxetine in patients with anorexia nervosa. J Clin Psychiatry 1991; 52:464–471 [G]

150. Levine JA, Eberhardt NL, Jensen MD: Role of nonexercise activity thermogenesis in resistance to fat gain in humans. Science 1999; 283:212–214 [B]

151. Baran SA, Weltzin TE, Kaye WH: Low discharge weight and outcome in anorexia nervosa. Am J Psychiatry 1995; 152:1070–1072 [C]

152. Halmi KA, Licinio-Paixao J: Outcome: hospital program for eating disorders, in 1989 Annual Meeting Syllabus and Proceedings Summary. Washington, DC, American Psychiatric Association, 1989, p 314 [G]

153. Agras WS: Eating Disorders: Management of Obesity, Bulimia and Anorexia Nervosa. Oxford, UK, Pergamon Press, 1987 [I]

154. Nusbaum JG, Drever E: Inpatient survey of nursing care measures for treatment of patients with anorexia nervosa. Issues Ment Health Nurs 1990; 11:175–184 [G]

155. Touyz SW, Beumont PJ, Glaun D, Phillips T, Cowie I: A comparison of lenient and strict operant conditioning programmes in refeeding patients with anorexia nervosa. Br J Psychiatry 1984; 144:517–520 [F]

156. Danziger Y, Carel CA, Tyano S, Mimouni M: Is psychotherapy mandatory during the actual refeeding period in the treatment of anorexia nervosa. J Adolesc Health Care 1989; 10:328–331 [B]

157. Duncan J, Kennedy SH: Inpatient group treatment, in Group Psychotherapy for Eating Disorders. Edited by Harper-Giuffre H, MacKenzie KR. Washington, DC, American Psychiatric Press, 1992, pp 149–160 [G]

158. Maxmen JS: Helping patients survive theories: the practice of an educative model. Int J Group Psychother 1984; 34:355–368 [G]

159. Yellowlees P: Group psychotherapy in anorexia nervosa. Int J Eat Disord 1988; 7:649–655 [G]

160. Maher MS: Group therapy for anorexia nervosa, in Current Treatment of Anorexia Nervosa and Bulimia. Edited by Powers PS, Fernandez RC. Basel, Switzerland, Karger, 1980, pp 265–276 [G]

161. Garner DM: Individual psychotherapy for anorexia nervosa. J Psychiatr Res 1985; 19:423–433 [F]

162. Hall A, Crisp AH: Brief psychotherapy in the treatment of anorexia nervosa: outcome at one year. Br J Psychiatry 1987; 151:185–191 [A]

163. Wilson CP, Mintz IL (eds): Psychosomatic Symptoms: Psychoanalytic Treatment of the Underlying Personality Disorder. Northvale, NJ, Jason Aronson, 1989 [F]

164. Dare C: The starving and the greedy. J Child Psychotherapy 1993; 19:3–22 [F]

165. Hornyak LM, Baker EK: Experiential Therapies for Eating Disorders. New York, Guilford Press, 1989 [G]

166. Breden AK: Occupational therapy and the treatment of eating disorders. Occupational Therapy in Health Care 1992; 8:49–68 [G]

167. Lim PY: Occupational therapy with eating disorders: a study on treatment approaches. Br J Occupational Therapy 1994; 57:309–314 [G]

168. Eisler I, Dare C, Russell G, Szmukler G, leGrange D, Dodge E: Family and individual therapy in anorexia nervosa: a 5-year follow-up. Arch Gen Psychiatry 1997; 54:1025–1030 [B]

169. Russell GF, Szmukler GI, Dare C, Eisler I: An evaluation of family therapy in anorexia nervosa and bulimia nervosa. Arch Gen Psychiatry 1987; 44:1047–1056 [A]

170. Agras WS, Hammer LD, McNicholas F: A prospective study of the influence of eating-disordered mothers on their children. Int J Eat Disord 1999; 25:253–262 [C]

171. Russell GF, Treasure J, Eisler I: Mothers with anorexia nervosa who underfeed their children: their recognition and management. Psychol Med 1998; 28:93–108 [D]

172. Stein A, Woolley H, Cooper SD, Fairburn CG: An observational study of mothers with eating disorders and their infants. J Child Psychol Psychiatry 1994; 35:733–748 [C]

173. Johnson CL, Taylor C: Working with difficult to treat eating disorders using an integration of twelve-step and traditional psychotherapies. Psychiatr Clin North Am 1996; 19:829–941 [F]

174. Fisher M, Golden NH, Katzman DK, Kreipe RE, Rees J, Schebendach J, Sigman G, Ammerman S, Hoberman HM: Eating disorders in adolescents: a background paper. J Adolesc Health 1995; 16:420–437 [F]

175. Attia E, Haiman C, Walsh BT, Flater SR: Does fluoxetine augment the inpatient treatment of anorexia nervosa? Am J Psychiatry 1998; 155:548–551 [A]

176. Gwirtsman HE, Guze BH, Yager J, Gainsley B: Fluoxetine treatment of anorexia nervosa: an open clinical trial. J Clin Psychiatry 1990; 51:378–382 [G]

177. Bergh C, Eriksson M, Lindberg G, Sodersten P: Selective serotonin reuptake inhibitors in anorexia. Lancet 1996; 348:1459–1460 [B]

178. Halmi KA, Eckert E, LaDu TJ, Cohen J: Anorexia nervosa: treatment efficacy of cyproheptadine and amitriptyline. Arch Gen Psychiatry 1986; 43:177–181 [A]

179. Lacey JH, Crisp AH: Hunger, food intake and weight: the impact of clomipramine on a refeeding anorexia nervosa population. Postgrad Med J 1980; 56(suppl 1):79–85 [A]

180. Gross HA, Ebert MH, Faden VB: A double-blind controlled study of lithium carbonate in primary anorexia nervosa. J Clin Psychopharmacol 1981; 1:376–381 [A]

181. Vandereycken W, Pierloot R: Pimozide combined with behavior therapy in the short-term treatment of anorexia nervosa: a double blind placebo-controlled cross-over study. Acta Psychiatr Scand 1982; 66:445–450 [A]

182. Wells LA, Logan KM: Pharmacologic treatment of eating disorders: a review of selected literature and recommendations. Psychosomatics 1987; 28:470–479 [F]

183. Garfinkel PE, Garner DM: Anorexia Nervosa: A Multidimensional Perspective. New York, Brunner/Mazel, 1982 [I]

184. Seeman E, Szmukler G, Formica C, Tsalamandris C, Mestrovic R: Osteoporosis in anorexia nervosa: the influence of peak bone density, bone loss, oral contraceptive use and exercise. J Bone Miner Res 1992; 7:1467–1474 [C]

185. Hegenroeder AC: Bone mineralization, hypothalamic amenorrhea, and sex steroid therapy in female adolescents and young adults. J Pediatr 1995; 126:683–689 [F]

186. Kreipe RE, Hicks DG, Rosier RN, Puzas JE: Preliminary findings on the effects of sex hormones on bone metabolism in anorexia nervosa. J Adolesc Health 1993; 14:319–324 [B]

187. Treasure JL, Russell GF, Fogelman I, Murby B: Reversible bone loss in anorexia nervosa. Br Med J (Clin Res Ed) 1987; 295:474–475 [D]

188. Emans SJ, Goldstein DP: Pediatric and Adolescent Gynecology, 3rd ed. Boston, Little, Brown, 1990 [G]

189. Grinspoon S, Baum H, Lee K, Anderson E, Herzog D, Klibanski A: Effects of short-term recombinant human insulin-like growth factor I administration on bone turnover in osteopenic women with anorexia nervosa. J Clin Endocrinol Metab 1996; 81:3864–3870 [B]

190. Physicians' Desk Reference, 46th ed. Montvale, NJ, Medical Economics, 1992 [G]

191. Horne RL, Ferguson JM, Pope HJ, Hudson JI, Lineberry CG, Ascher J, Cato A: Treatment of bulimia with bupropion: a multicenter controlled trial. J Clin Psychiatry 1988; 49:262–266 [A]

192. Laessle RG, Zoettle C, Pirke KM: Meta-analysis of treatment studies for bulimia. Int J Eat Disord 1987; 6:647–654 [E]

193. Agras WS, Schneider JA, Arnow B, Raeburn SD, Telch CF: Cognitive-behavioral and response prevention treatments for bulimia nervosa. J Consult Clin Psychol 1989; 57:215–221 [A]

194. Beck AT, Ward CH, Mendelson M, Mock J, Erbaugh J: An inventory for measuring depression. Arch Gen Psychiatry 1961; 4:561–571 [G]

195. Connors ME, Johnson CL, Stuckey MK: Treatment of bulimia with brief psychoeducational group therapy. Am J Psychiatry 1984; 141:1512–1516 [B]

196. Fairburn CG, Jones R, Peveler RC, Hope RA, O'Connor M: Psychotherapy and bulimia nervosa: longer-term effects of interpersonal psychotherapy, behavior therapy, and cognitive behavioral therapy. Arch Gen Psychiatry 1993; 50:419–428 [A]

197. Fairburn CG, Marcus MD, Wilson GT: Cognitive-behavioral therapy for binge eating and bulimia nervosa: a comprehensive treatment manual, in Binge Eating: Nature, Assessment, and Treatment. Edited by Fairburn CG, Wilson GT. New York, Guilford Press, 1993, pp 361–404 [G]

198. Freeman CP, Barry F, Dunkeld-Turnbull J, Henderson A: Controlled trial of psychotherapy for bulimia nervosa. Br Med J (Clin Res Ed) 1988; 296:521–525 [B]

199. Garner DM, Rockert W, Davis R, Garner MV, Olmsted MP, Eagle M: A comparison of cognitive-behavioral and supportive-expressive therapy for bulimia nervosa. Am J Psychiatry 1993; 150:37–46 [B]

200. Hamilton M: A rating scale for depression. J Neurol Neurosurg Psychiatry 1960; 23:56–62 [D]

201. Kirkley BG, Schneider JA, Agras WS, Bachman JA: Comparison of two group treatments for bulimia. J Consult Clin Psychol 1985; 53:43–48 [A]

202. Lee NF, Rush AJ: Cognitive-behavioral group therapy for bulimia. Int J Eat Disord 1986; 5:599–615 [A]

203. Malenbaum R, Herzog D, Eisenthal S, Wyshak G: Overeaters anonymous. Int J Eat Disord 1988; 7:139–144 [G]

204. Mitchell JE, Pyle RL, Pomeroy C, Zollman M, Crosby R, Sein H, Eckert ED, Zimmerman R: Cognitive-behavioral group psychotherapy of bulimia nervosa: importance of logistical variables. Int J Eat Disord 1993; 14:277–287 [B]

205. Oesterheld JR, McKenna MS, Gould NB: Group psychotherapy of bulimia: a critical review. Int J Group Psychother 1987; 37:163–184 [F]

206. Ordman AM, Kirschenbaum DS: Cognitive-behavioral therapy for bulimia: an initial outcome study. J Consult Clin Psychol 1985; 53:305–313 [B]

207. Schwartz RC, Barett MJ, Saba G: Family therapy for bulimia, in Handbook of Psychotherapy for Anorexia Nervosa and Bulimia. Edited by Garner DM, Garfinkel PE. New York, Guilford Press, 1985, pp 280–307 [G]

208. Vandereycken W: The addiction model in eating disorders: some critical remarks and a selected bibliography. Int J Eat Disord 1990; 9:95–102 [G]

209. Yager J, Landsverk J, Edelstein CK: Help seeking and satisfaction with care in 641 women with eating disorders I: patterns of utilization attributed change and perceived efficacy of treatment. J Nerv Ment Dis 1989; 177:632–637 [G]

210. Beck AT, Steer RA, Garbin MG: Psychometric properties of the BDI: twenty-five years of evaluation. Clin Psychol Rev 1988; 8:77–100 [G]

211. Root MPP: Persistent, disordered eating as a gender-specific, post-traumatic stress response to sexual assault. Psychotherapy 1991; 28:96–102 [G]

212. Laessle RG, Tuschl RJ, Kotthaus BC, Pirke JM: A comparison of the validity of three scales for the assessment of dietary restraint. J Abnorm Psychol 1989; 98:504–507 [E]

213. Fairburn CG: Cognitive behavioral treatment for bulimia, in Handbook of Psychotherapy for Anorexia Nervosa and Bulimia. Edited by Garner DM, Garfinkel PE. New York, Guilford Press, 1985, pp 160–192 [G]

214. Fairburn CG, Kirk J, O'Connor M, Cooper PJ: A comparison of two psychological treatments for bulimia nervosa. Behav Res Ther 1985; 24:629–643 [B]

215. Leitenberg H, Rosen J, Gross J, Nudelman S, Vara LS: Exposure plus response-prevention treatment of bulimia nervosa. J Consult Clin Psychol 1988; 56:535–541 [A]

216. Johnson C: Diagnostic survey for eating disorders in initial consultation for patients with bulimia and anorexia nervosa, in Handbook of Psychotherapy for Anorexia

Nervosa and Bulimia. Edited by Garner DM, Garfinkel PE. New York, Guilford Press, 1985, pp 19–51 [G]

217. Fairburn CG: A cognitive behavioral approach to the treatment of bulimia. Psychol Med 1981; 11:707–711 [B]

218. Fairburn CG, Norman PA, Welch SL, O'Conner ME, Doll HA, Peveler RC: A prospective study of outcome in bulimia nervosa and the long-term effects of three psychological treatments. Arch Gen Psychiatry 1995; 52:304–312 [A]

219. Rorty M, Yager J: Why and how do women recover from bulimia nervosa? Int J Eat Disord 1993; 14:249–260 [D]

220. Fairburn CG, Jones R, Peveler RC: Three psychological treatments for bulimia nervosa. Arch Gen Psychiatry 1991; 48:453–469 [A]

221. Wilson GT, Eldredge KL, Smith D: Cognitive behavioral treatment with and without response prevention for bulimia. Behav Res Ther 1991; 29:575–583 [A]

222. Wilson GT, Rossiter E, Kleifield EI, Lindholm L: Cognitive-behavioral treatment of bulimia nervosa: a controlled evaluation. Behav Res Ther 1986; 24:277–288 [B]

223. Cooper PJ, Coker S, Fleming C: Self-help for bulimia nervosa: a preliminary report. Int J Eat Disord 1994; 16:401–404 [B]

224. Cooper PJ, Coker S, Fleming C: An evaluation of the efficacy of supervised cognitive behavioral self-help for bulimia nervosa. J Psychosom Res 1996; 40:281–287 [B]

225. Thiels C, Schmidt U, Treasure J, Garthe R, Troop N: Guided self-change for bulimia nervosa incorporating use of a self-care manual. Am J Psychiatry 1998; 155:947–953 [B]

226. Treasure J, Schmidt U, Troop N, Tiller J, Todd G, Keilen M, Dodge E: First step in managing bulimia nervosa: controlled trial of therapeutic manual. Br Med J 1994; 308:686–689 [B]

227. Treasure J, Schmidt U, Troop N, Tiller J, Todd G, Turnbull S: Sequential treatment for bulimia nervosa incorporating a self-care manual. Br J Psychiatry 1995; 167:1–5 [B]

228. Agras WS: Cognitive Behavior Therapy Treatment Manual for Bulimia Nervosa. Stanford, Calif, Stanford University School of Medicine, Department of Psychiatry and Behavioral Sciences, 1991 [F]

229. Agras WS, Apple R: Overcoming Eating Disorders—Therapist's Guide. San Antonio, Tex, Psychological Corp (Harcourt), 1998 [G]

230. Apple R, Agras WS: Overcoming Eating Disorders—Client Workbook. San Antonio, Tex, Psychological Corp (Harcourt), 1998 [G]

231. Boutacoff LI, Zollman M, Mitchell JE: Healthy Eating: A Meal Planning System—Group Treatment Manual. Minneapolis, University of Minnesota Hospital and Clinic, Department of Psychiatry, 1989 [G]

232. Mitchell JE, Eating Disorders Program Staff: Bulimia Nervosa: Individual Treatment Manual. Minneapolis, University of Minnesota Hospital and Clinic, Department of Psychiatry, 1989 [F]

233. Mitchell JE, Eating Disorders Program Staff: Bulimia Nervosa: Group Treatment Manual. Minneapolis, University of Minnesota Hospital and Clinic, Department of Psychiatry, 1991 [F]

234. Pope HG Jr, Hudson JI, Jonas JM, Yurgelun-Todd D: Bulimia treated with imipramine: a placebo-controlled, double-blind study. Am J Psychiatry 1983; 140:554–558 [A]

235. Hughes PL, Wells LA, Cunningham CJ, Ilstrup DM: Treating bulimia with desipramine: a double-blind placebo-controlled study. Arch Gen Psychiatry 1986; 43:182–186 [A]

236. Mitchell JE, Groat R: A placebo-controlled double-blind trial of amitriptyline in bulimia. J Clin Psychopharmacol 1984; 4:186–193 [A]

237. Walsh BT, Stewart JW, Roose SP, Gladis M, Glassman AH: Treatment of bulimia with phenelzine: a double-blind placebo controlled study. Arch Gen Psychiatry 1984; 41:1105–1109 [A]

238. Alger SA, Schwalberg MD, Bigaoutte JM, Michalek AV, Howard LJ: Effects of a tricyclic antidepressant and opiate antagonists on binge-eating behavior in normal weight bulimic and obese binge-eating subjects. J Clin Nutr 1991; 53:865–871 [A]

239. Fahy TA, Eisler I, Russell GFM: A placebo-controlled trial of d-fenfluramine in bulimia nervosa. Br J Psychiatry 1993; 162:597–603 [B]

240. Fichter MM, Kruger R, Rief W, Holland R, Dohne J: Fluvoxamine in prevention of relapse in bulimia nervosa: effects on eating-specific psychopathology. J Clin Psychopharmacol 1996; 16:9–18 [A]

241. Fichter MM, Leibl K, Rief W, Brunner E, Schmidt-Auberger S, Engel RR: Fluoxetine versus placebo: a double-blind study with bulimic inpatients undergoing intensive psychotherapy. Pharmacopsychiatry 1991; 24:1–7 [A]

242. Fluoxetine Bulimia Nervosa Collaborative Study Group: Fluoxetine in the treatment of bulimia nervosa. Arch Gen Psychiatry 1992; 49:139–147 [A]

243. Freeman CP, Morris JE, Cheshire KE, Davies F, Hamson M: A double-blind controlled trial of fluoxetine versus placebo for bulimia nervosa. Proceedings of the Third International Conference on Eating Disorders, New York, 1988 [A]

244. Goldstein DJ, Wilson MG, Thompson VL, Potvin JH, Rampey AH Jr (Fluoxetine Bulimia Nervosa Research Group): Long-term fluoxetine treatment of bulimia nervosa. Br J Psychiatry 1995; 166:660–666 [A]

245. Hsu LKG, Clement L, Santhouse R, Ju ESY: Treatment of bulimia nervosa with lithium carbonate: a controlled study. J Nerv Ment Dis 1991; 179:351–355 [A]

246. Igoin-Apfelbaum L, Apfelbaum M: Naltrexone and bulimic symptoms (letter). Lancet 1987; 2:1087–1088 [A]

247. Jonas JM, Gold MS: Naltrexone reverses bulimic symptoms (letter). Lancet 1986; 1:807 [G]

248. Jonas JM, Gold MS: Treatment of antidepressant-resistant bulimia with naltrexone. Int J Psychiatry Med 1986; 16:306–309 [B]

249. Mitchell JE, Christenson G, Jennings J, Huber M, Thomas B, Pomeroy C, Morley J: A placebo-controlled double-blind crossover study of naltrexone hydrochloride in outpatients with normal weight bulimia. J Clin Psychopharmacol 1989; 9:94–97 [A]

250. Pope HG Jr, Keck PE Jr, McElroy SL, Hudson JI: A placebo-controlled study of trazodone in bulimia nervosa. J Clin Psychopharmacol 1989; 9:254–259 [A]

251. Rothschild R, Quitkin HM, Quitkin FM, Stewart JW, Ocepek-Welikson K, McGrath PJ, Tricamo E: A double-blind placebo-controlled comparison of phenelzine and imipramine in the treatment of bulimia in atypical depressives. Int J Eat Disord 1994; 15:1–9 [A]

252. Sabine EJ, Yonace A, Farrington AJ, Barratt KH, Wakeling A: Bulimia nervosa: a placebo-controlled double-blind therapeutic trial of mianserin. Br J Clin Pharmacol 1983; 15:195S–202S [A]

253. Agras WS, Dorian B, Kirkley BG, Arnow B, Bachman J: Imipramine in the treatment of bulimia: a double-blind controlled study. Int J Eat Disord 1987; 6:29–38 [A]

254. Barlow J, Blouin J, Blouin A, Perez E: Treatment of bulimia with desipramine: a double blind crossover study. Can J Psychiatry 1988; 33:129–133 [A]

255. Blouin AG, Blouin JH, Perez EL, Bushnik T, Zuro C, Mulder E: Treatment of bulimia with fenfluramine and desipramine. J Clin Psychopharmacol 1988; 8:261–269 [A]

256. Walsh BT, Hadigan CM, Devlin MJ, Gladis M, Roose SP: Long-term outcome of antidepressant treatment for bulimia nervosa. Am J Psychiatry 1991; 148:1206–1212 [A]

257. Kennedy SH, Piran N, Warsh JJ, Prendergast P, Mainprize E, Whynot C, Garfinkel PE: A trial of isocarboxacid in the treatment of bulimia nervosa. J Clin Psychopharmacol 1988; 8:391–396; correction, 1989; 9:3 [A]

258. Kennedy SH, Goldbloom DS, Ralevski E, Davis C, D'Souza JD, Lofchy J: Is there a role for selective monoamine oxidase inhibitor therapy in bulimia nervosa? a placebo-controlled trial of brofaromine. J Clin Psychopharmacol 1993; 13:415–422 [A]

259. Raymond NC, Mitchell JE, Fallon P, Katzman MA: A collaborative approach to the use of medication, in Feminist Perspectives on Eating Disorders. Edited by Fallon P, Katzman MA, Wooley SC. New York, Guilford Press, 1994, pp 231–250 [G]

260. Marrazzi MA, Wroblewski JM, Kinzie J, Luby ED: High dose naltrexone in eating disorders—liver function data. Am J Addict 1997; 6:621–629 [B]

261. Mitchell JE, Pyle RL, Eckert ED, Hatsukami D, Zimmerman R, Pomeroy C: A comparison study of antidepressants and structured intensive group psychotherapy in the treatment of bulimia nervosa. Arch Gen Psychiatry 1990; 47:149–157 [A]

262. Agras WS, Rossiter EM, Arnow B, Schneider JA, Telch CF, Raeburn SD, Bruce B, Perl M, Koran LM: Pharmacologic and cognitive-behavioral treatment for bulimia nervosa: a controlled comparison. Am J Psychiatry 1992; 149:82–87 [A]

263. Goldbloom DS, Olmsted M, Davis R, Clewes J, Heinmaa M, Rockert W, Shaw B: A randomized controlled trial of fluoxetine and cognitive behavioral therapy for bulimia nervosa: short-term outcome. Behav Res Ther 1997; 35:803–811 [A]

264. Walsh BT, Wilson GT, Loeb KL, Devlin MJ, Pike KM, Roose SP, Fleiss J, Waternaux C: Medication and psychotherapy in the treatment of bulimia nervosa. Am J Psychiatry 1997; 154:523–531 [G]

265. Leitenberg H, Rosen JC, Wolf J, Vara LS, Detzer MJ, Srebnik D: Comparison of cognitive-behavior therapy and desipramine in the treatment of bulimia nervosa. Behav Res Ther 1994; 32:37–45 [A]

266. Spitzer RL, Devlin MJ, Walsh BT, Hasin D: Binge eating disorder: a multisite field trial of the diagnostic criteria. Int J Eat Disord 1992; 11:191–203 [D]

267. de Zwaan M, Mitchell JE, Mussell MP, Crosby RD: Does CBT improve outcomes in obese binge eaters participating in a very low-calorie diet treatment? Presented at the Eating Disorders Research Society annual meeting, Pittsburgh, PA, November 15–17, 1996 [B]

268. Telch CF, Agras WS: The effects of a very low calorie diet on binge eating. Behavior Therapy 1993; 24:177–193 [B]

269. Wadden TA, Foster GD, Letizia KA: Response of obese binge eaters to treatment by behavior therapy combined with very low calorie diet. J Consult Clin Psychol 1992; 60:808–811 [A]

270. Yanovski SZ, Gormally JF, Leser MS, Gwirtsman HE, Yanovski JA: Binge eating disorder affects outcome of comprehensive very-low-calorie diet treatment. Obesity Res 1994; 2:205–212 [B]

271. Polivy J, Herman CP: Dieting and binging: a casual analysis. Am Psychol 1985; 40:193–201 [F]

272. Carrier KM, Steinhardt MA, Bowman S: Rethinking traditional weight management programs: a 3-year follow-up evaluation of a new approach. J Psychol 1993; 128:517–535 [D]

273. Ciliska D: Beyond Dieting: Psychoeducational Interventions for Chronically Obese Women. New York, Brunner/Mazel, 1990 [G]

274. Kaplan AS, Ciliska D: The relationship between eating disorders and obesity: psychopathologic and treatment considerations. Psychiatr Annals 1999; 29:197–202 [B]

275. Goodrick GK, Poston WS II, Kimball KT, Reeves RS, Foreyt JP: Nondieting versus dieting treatment of overweight binge-eating women. J Consult Clin Psychol 1998; 66:363–368 [B]

276. Tanco S, Linden W, Earle T: Well-being and morbid obesity in women: a controlled therapy evaluation. Int J Eat Disord 1998; 23:325–339 [B]

277. Grilo CM: Treatment of obesity: an integrative model, in Body Image, Eating Disorders, and Obesity. Edited by Thompson JK. Washington, DC, American Psychological Association, 1996, pp 389–423 [G]

278. Marcus MD: Obese patients with binge-eating disorder, in The Management of Eating Disorders and Obesity. Edited by Goldstein DJ. Totowa, NJ, Humana Press, 1999, pp 125–138 [G]

279. Agras WS, Telch CF, Arnow B, Eldredge K, Detzer MJ, Henderson J, Marnell M: Does interpersonal therapy help patients with binge-eating disorder who fail to respond to cognitive-behavioral therapy? J Consult Clin Psychol 1995; 63:356–360 [B]

280. Agras WS, Telch CF, Arnow B, Eldredge K, Wilfley DE, Raeburn SD, Henderson S, Marnell M: Weight loss cognitive-behavioral and desipramine treatments in binge-eating disorder: an addictive design. Behavior Therapy 1994; 25:225–238 [A]

281. Carter FA, Bulik CM, Lawson RH, Sullivan PF, Wilson JS: Effect of mood and food cues on body image in women with bulimia and controls. Int J Eat Disord 1996; 20:65–76 [B]

282. Eldredge KL, Agras WS, Arnow B, Telch CF, Bell S, Castonguay L, Marnell M: The effects of extending cognitive-behavioral therapy for binge eating disorder among initial treatment nonresponders. Int J Eat Disord 1999; 21:347–352 [B]

283. Marcus MD, Wing RR: Cognitive treatment of binge eating, V: behavioral weight control in the treatment of binge eating disorder (letter). Ann Behav Med 1995; 17:S090 [A]

284. Peterson C, Mitchell JM, Engbloom S, Nugent S, Mussell MP, Miller JP: Group cognitive-behavioral treatment of binge eating disorder: a comparison of therapist-led versus self-help formats. Int J Eat Disord 1998; 24:125–136 [B]

285. Smith DE, Marcus MD, Kaye W: Cognitive-behavioral treatment of obese binge eaters. Int J Eat Disord 1992; 12:257–262 [B]

286. Telch CF, Agras WS, Rossiter EM, Wilfey D, Kenardy J: Group cognitive-behavioral treatment for the nonpurging bulimic: an initial evaluation. J Consult Clin Psychol 1990; 58:629–635 [B]

287. Wilfey DE, Agras WS, Telch CF, Rossiter EM, Schneider JA, Cole AG, Sifford LA, Raeburn SD: Group cognitive-behavioral therapy and group interpersonal psychotherapy for the nonpurging bulimic individual: a controlled comparison. J Consult Clin Psychol 1993; 61:296–305 [A]

288. Fichter MM, Quadflieg N, Gnutmann A: Binge-eating disorder: treatment outcome over a 6-year course. J Psychosom Res 1998; 44:385–405 [E]

289. Carter JC, Fairburn CG: Cognitive-behavioral self-help for binge eating disorder: a controlled effectiveness study. J Consult Clin Psychol 1998; 66:616–623 [B]

290. Stunkard A, Berkowitz R, Tanrikut C, Reiss E, Young L: d-Fenfluramine treatment of binge eating disorder. Am J Psychiatry 1996; 153:1455–1459 [A]

291. Gardiner HM, Freeman CP, Jesinger DK, Collins SA: Fluvoxamine: an open pilot study in moderately obese female patients suffering from atypical eating disorders and episodes of bingeing. Int J Obes Relat Metab Disord 1993; 17:301–305 [B]

292. Hudson JI, McElroy SL, Raymond NC, Crow S, Keck PE Jr, Carter WP, Mitchell JE, Strakowski SM, Pope HG Jr, Coleman BS, Jonas JM: Fluvoxamine in the treatment of binge-eating disorder: a multicenter placebo-controlled, double-blind trial. Am J Psychiatry 1998; 155:1756–1762 [A]

293. McCann UD, Agras WS: Successful treatment of nonpurging bulimia nervosa with desipramine: a double-blind, placebo-controlled study. Am J Psychiatry 1990; 147:1509–1513 [A]

294. Abenhaim L, Moride Y, Brenot F, Rich S, Benichou J, Kurz X, Higenbottam T, Oakley C, Wouters E, Aubier M, Simonneau G, Beguad B: Appetite-suppressant drugs and the risk of primary pulmonary hypertension. N Engl J Med 1996; 335:609–616 [D]

295. Connolly H, Crary J, McGoon M, Hensrud D, Edwards B, Edwards W, Schaff H: Valvular heart disease associated with fenfluramine-phentermine. N Engl J Med 1997; 337:581–588 [C]

296. Graham DJ, Green L: Further cases of valvular heart disease associated with fenfluramine-phentermine (letter). N Engl J Med 1997; 337:635 [G]

297. Mark EJ, Patalas ED, Chang HT, Evans RJ, Kessler SC: Fatal pulmonary hypertension associated with short-term use of fenfluramine and phentermine. N Engl J Med 1997; 337:602–606 [G]

298. McCann U, Hatzidimitriou G, Ridenour A, Fischer C, Yuan J, Katz J, Ricaurte G: Dexfenfluramine and serotonin neurotoxicity: further preclinical evidence that clinical caution is indicated. J Pharmacol Exp Ther 1994; 269:792–798 [G]

299. Ricaurte GA, Martello MB, Wilson MA, Molliver ME, Katz JL, Martello AL: Dexfenfluramine neurotoxicity in brains of non-human primates. Lancet 1991; 338:1487–1488 [G]

300. Marcus MD, Wing RR, Ewing L, Kern E, McDermott M, Gooding W: A double-blind, placebo-controlled trial of fluoxetine plus behavior modification in the treatment of obese binge-eaters and non-binge-eaters. Am J Psychiatry 1990; 147:876–881 [A]

301. Kerr A, Leszcz M, Kaplan AS: Continuing care groups for chronic anorexia nervosa, in Group Psychotherapy for Eating Disorders. Edited by Harper-Giuffre H, MacKenzie KR. Washington, DC, American Psychiatric Press, 1992, pp 261–272 [G]

302. Holderness C, Brooks-Gunn J, Warren M: Comorbidity of eating disorders and substance abuse: review of the literature. Int J Eat Disord 1994; 16:1–35 [F]

303. Bulik C, Sullivan P, Epstein L, McKee M, Kaye W, Dahl R, Weltzin T: Drug use in women with anorexia and bulimia nervosa. Int J Eat Disord 1992; 11:214–225 [D]

304. Bulik C, Sullivan P, Fear J, Pickering A, Dawn A, McCullin M: Fertility and reproduction in women with anorexia nervosa: a controlled study. J Clin Psychiatry 1999; 60:130–135 [B]

305. Strober M, Freeman R, Bower S, Rigali J: Binge-eating in anorexia nervosa predicts later onset of substance use disorder: a ten-year prospective, longitudinal follow-up of 95 adolescents. J Youth and Adolescence 1997; 25:519–532 [C]

306. Hatsukami D, Mitchell JE, Eckert E, Pyle R: Characteristics of patients with bulimia only, bulimia with affective disorder and bulimia with substance abuse problems. Addict Behav 1986; 11:399–406 [D]

307. Collings S, King M: Ten year follow-up of 50 patients with bulimia nervosa. Br J Psychiatry 1994; 165:80–87 [C]

308. Mitchell JE, Pyle RL, Eckert ED, Hatsukami D: The influence of prior alcohol and drug abuse problems on bulimia nervosa treatment outcome. Addict Behav 1990; 15:169–173 [D]

309. Strasser T, Pike K, Walsh B: The impact of prior substance abuse on treatment outcome for bulimia nervosa. Addict Behav 1992; 17:387–395 [C]

310. Westermeyer J, Specker S: Social resources and social function in comorbid eating and substance disorder: a matched-pairs study. Am J Addict (in press) [A]

311. Cooper PJ: Eating disorders and their relationship to mood and anxiety disorders, in Eating Disorders and Obesity: A Comprehensive Handbook. Edited by Brownell KD, Fairburn CG. New York, Guilford Press, 1995, pp 159–164 [G]

312. Edelstein CK, Yager J: Eating disorders and affective disorders, in Special Problems in Managing Eating Disorders. Edited by Yager J, Gwirtsman HE, Edelstein CK. Washington, DC, American Psychiatric Press, 1992, pp 15–50 [G]

313. Cooper PJ, Fairburn GG: The depressive symptoms of bulimia nervosa. Br J Psychiatry 1986; 148:268–274 [G]

314. Bulik C, Sullivan P, Fear J, Joyce PR: Eating disorders and antecedent anxiety disorders: a controlled study. Acta Psychiatr Scand 1997; 92:101–107 [B]

315. Bulik CM, Sullivan PF, Joyce PR, Carter FA: Temperament, character, personality disorder in bulimia nervosa. J Nerv Ment Dis 1995; 183:593–598 [B]

316. Johnson C, Tobin D, Enright A: Prevalence and clinical characteristics of borderline patients in an eating disordered population. J Clin Psychiatry 1989; 50:9–15 [D]

317. Vitousek K, Manke F: Personality variables and disorders in anorexia nervosa and bulimia nervosa. J Abnorm Psychol 1994; 103:137–147 [G]

318. Wonderlich SA: Personality and eating disorders, in Eating Disorders and Obesity: A Comprehensive Textbook. Edited by Brownell KD, Fairburn C. New York, Guilford Press, 1996, pp 171–176 [G]

319. Wonderlich SA, Mitchell JE: Eating disorders and personality disorders, in Special Problems in Managing Eating Disorders. Edited by Yager J, Gwirtsman HE, Edelstein CK. Washington, DC, American Psychiatric Press, 1992, pp 51–86 [G]

320. Wonderlich SA, Swift WJ: Borderline versus other personality disorders in the eating disorders: clinical description. Int J Eat Disord 1990; 9:629–638 [G]

321. Ames-Frankel J, Devlin MJ, Walsh BT, Strasser TJ, Sadik C, Oldham JM, Roose SP: Personality disorder diagnoses in patients with bulimia nervosa: clinical correlates and changes with treatment. J Clin Psychiatry 1992; 53:90–96 [C]

322. Johnson C, Tobin DL, Dennis A: Differences in treatment outcome between borderline and non-borderline bulimics at one-year follow-up. Int J Eat Disord 1990; 9:617–627 [B]

323. Dansky BS, Brewerton TD, Kilpatrick DG, O'Neil PM: The National Women's Study: relationship of victimization and posttraumatic stress disorder to bulimia nervosa. Int J Eat Disord 1997; 21:213–228 [D]

324. Rodin G, Daneman D, DeGroot J: The interaction of chronic medical illness and eating disorders, in Medical Issues and the Eating Disorders: The Interface. Edited by Kaplan AS, Garfinkel PE. New York, Brunner/Mazel, 1993, pp 179–181 [G]

325. Yager J, Young RT: Eating disorders and diabetes mellitus, in Special Problems in Managing Eating Disorders. Edited by Yager J, Gwirtsman HE, Edelstein CK. Washington, DC, American Psychiatric Press, 1992, pp 185–203 [G]

326. Powers PS: Management of patients with comorbid medical conditions, in Handbook of Treatment for Eating Disorders, 2nd ed. Edited by Garner DM, Garfinkel PE. New York, Guilford Press, 1997, pp 424–436 [G]

327. Brinch M, Isageer T, Tolstrup K: Anorexia nervosa and motherhood: reproduction pattern and mothering behavior of 50 women. Acta Psychiatr Scand 1988; 77:611–617 [C]

328. Rand CSW, Willis DC, Kuldau JM: Pregnancy after anorexia nervosa. Int J Eat Disord 1987; 6:671–674 [G]

329. Stewart DE, Raskin J, Garfinkel PE, MacDonald OL, Robinson GE: Anorexia nervosa, bulimia and pregnancy. Am J Obstet Gynecol 1987; 157:1194–1198 [C]

330. Treasure JL, Russell GF: Intrauterine growth and neonatal weight gain in babies of women with anorexia nervosa. Br Med J 1988; 296:1038–1039 [B]

331. Lacey H, Smith G: Bulimia nervosa: the impact of pregnancy on mother and baby. Br J Psychiatry 1987; 150:777–781 [D]

332. Powers PS, Spratt EG: Males and females with eating disorders. Eating Disorders: J Treatment and Prevention 1994; 2:197–214 [D]

333. Carlat DJ, Camargo CA Jr, Herzog DB: Eating disorders in males: a report on 135 patients. Am J Psychiatry 1997; 154:1127–1132 [G]

334. Fichter MM, Daser CC: Symptomatology, psychosexual development, and gender identity in 42 anorexic males. Psychol Med 1987; 17:409–418 [G]

335. Andersen AE: Males With Eating Disorders. New York, Brunner/Mazel, 1990 [G]

336. Golden NH, Kreitzer P, Jacobson MS, Chasalow FI, Schebendach J, Freedman SM, Shenker IR: Disturbances in growth hormone secretion and action in adolescents with anorexia nervosa. J Pediatr 1994; 125:655–660 [D]

337. Katzman DK, Zipursky RB: Adolescents with anorexia nervosa: the impact of the disorder on bones and brains. Ann NY Acad Sci 1997; 817:127–137 [F]

338. Katzman DK, Zipursky RB, Lambe EK, Mikulis DJ: A longitudinal magnetic resonance imaging study of brain changes in adolescents with anorexia nervosa. Arch Pediatr Adolesc Med 1997; 151:793–797 [C]

339. Nussbaum MP, Baird D, Sonnenblick M, Cowan K, Shenker IR: Short stature in anorexia nervosa patients. J Adolesc Health Care 1985; 6:453–455 [D]

340. Pfeiffer RJ, Lucas AR, Ilstrup DM: Effects of anorexia nervosa on linear growth. Clin Pediatr (Phila) 1986; 25:7–12 [G]

341. Henry MC, Perlmutter SJ, Swedo SE: Anorexia, OCD, and streptococcus. J Am Acad Child Adolesc Psychiatry 1999; 38:228–229 [G]

342. Sokol MS, Gray NS: Case study: an infection triggered, autoimmune subtype of anorexia nervosa. J Am Acad Child Adolesc Psychiatry 1997; 36:1128–1133 [G]

343. Gupta MA: Concerns about aging and a drive for thinness: a factor in the biopsychosocial model of eating disorders? Int J Eat Disord 1995; 18:351–357 [B]

344. Boast N, Coker E, Wakeling A: Anorexia nervosa of late onset. Br J Psychiatry 1992; 160:257–260 [G]

345. Davis C, Yager J: Transcultural aspects of eating disorders: a critical literature review. Cult Med Psychiatry 1992; 16:377–382 [G]

346. Katzman MA, Lee S: Beyond body image: the integration of feminist and transcultural theories in the understanding of self-starvation. Int J Eat Disord 1997; 22:385–394 [F]

347. Powers PS, Johnson C: Small victories: prevention of eating disorders among athletes. Eating Disorders: J Treatment and Prevention 1997; 4:364–377 [D]

348. Thompson RA, Sherman RT: Helping Athletes With Eating Disorders. Champaign, Ill, Human Kinetics, 1993 [G]

349. Williamson DA, Netemeyer RG, Jackman LP, Anderson DA, Funsch CL, Rabalais JY: Structural equation modeling for risk factors for the development of eating disorder symptoms in female athletes. Int J Eat Disord 1995; 17:387–393 [E]

350. Nattiv A, Agostini R, Drinkwater B, Yeager KK: The female athlete triad: the interrelatedness of disordered eating, amenorrhea, and osteoporosis. Clin Sports Med 1994; 13:405–418 [G]

351. Yates A: Athletes, eating disorders and the overtraining syndrome, in Activity Anorexia: Theory, Research and Treatment. Edited by Epling W, Pierce W. Hillsdale, NJ, Lawrence Erlbaum Associates, 1996, pp 179–188 [G]

352. Epling W, Pierce W: Activity Anorexia: Theory, Research, Treatment. Hillsdale, NJ, Lawrence Erlbaum Associates, 1996 [G]

353. Mann T, Nolen-Hoeksema S, Huang K, Burgard D, Wright A, Hanson K: Are two interventions worse than none? joint primary and secondary prevention of eating disorders in college females. Health Psychol 1997; 16:215–225 [B]

354. Shisslak CM, Crago M, Estes LS, Gray N: Content and method of developmentally appropriate prevention programs, in The Developmental Psychopathology of Eating Disorders: Implications for Research, Prevention, and Treatment. Edited by Smolak L, Levine MP, Striegel-Moore RH. Mahwah, NJ, Lawrence Erlbaum Associates, 1996, pp 341–363 [E]

355. Glenn AA, Pollard JW, Denovcheck JA, Smith AF: Eating disorders on campus: a procedure for community intervention. J Counseling & Development 1986; 65:163–165 [G]

356. Coll KM: Mandatory psychiatric withdrawal from public colleges and universities: a review of potential legal violations and appropriate use. J College Student Psychotherapy 1991; 5:91–98 [E]